To Judy & Scott on your
40th Wedding Anniversary
from your Scottish Friends
in Guernsey

Moira & Graham

With Love.

The Cotentin *and* *Channel* Islands

An extraordinary archipelago

OCEAN OCCIDENTAL

AURIGNY aux Anglois ORNY I.

Anse de Vauville

GRENEZEY ou GUERNEZE I.

HERMS I.

Cers I.

MER BRITANNIQUE.

GERZEY ou JERSAY I.

Rochers d'Ecrehou

Banes Grelets

Les Minquiers

ISLES DE CHAUSEY

Unelli seu Veneli

DIOCESE DE COUTANCES

DIVISÉ EN SES QUATRE ARCHIDIACONES,
et vint-deux Doiennés Ruraux
avec les Isles de
IERSAY, GRENESEY, CERS, HERMS, AURIGNI etc.
Dedié a
Monseigneur l'Illustrissime, et Reverendissime Charles-Francois de
Lomenie de Brienne, Evêque de Coutances.

Par son tres humble, et tres obeissant serviteur
G. MARIETTE   DE LA PAGERIE

NOTES, ET   ABBREVIATIONS

ÉCHELLE

A Paris chez I. Mariette
rue St. Iacques à la Victoire et aux Colonnes d'Hercules.
Avec Privilege du Roy.

S. Malo   BRETAGNE

RADE DE CANCALE

Cancale

La Manche ou le Canal autrement Mer Britannique

This beautiful map, drawn by G. Mariette de la Pagerie, dates from 1689. It illustrates, not only the French isles bordering the Cotentin, from the Mont Saint-Michel to the west, to the Saint-Marcouf Islands to the east, but also the islands of Alderney, Guernsey, Herm, Sark and Jersey, together with the reefs of the Ecrehou and the Minquiers. These English islands, a little too close for comfort, were for a long time at the heart of the concerns of the king's officers' and engineers' in charge of defending the French coasts.

The « Martello » towers, erected 89 years later to defend the coasts of Jersey and Guernsey (see below tower N°6, in L'Ancress Bay in Guernsey), are reminders of the permanent fear among the islanders, particularly strong throughout the 18th and up to the mid 19th Century, of seeing their islands subjected to invasion attempts by the French.

The Pointe Robert lighthouse
in Sark.

Prologue

Who has never dreamt of discovering an island? Islands always exert the same intriguing magnetism, particularly when you can barely make them out, those mysterious and unknown worlds, home to pirates or treasure, or even deserted, the subjects of so many of my childhood fantasies, from my own homeland, the Cotentin peninsula. At a very early age, I decided to discover the strange rocks which punctuated our maritime horizon. First of all as a teenager, in a centre boarder for the closest – Tatihou and the two Saint-Marcouf islands - then aboard a habitable sailboat, navigating through the terrible Raz Blanchard or Race of Alderney, to reach the island of the same name. From then on, the road was wide open to discover the entire Channel Island archipelago, those isles which we lost after many a trial and tribulation following Normandy's occupation by the French, as early as 1204, under Philip Augustus' reign!

From my very first childhood discoveries onwards, I have often travelled across these islands, each and every time with renewed delight in discovering once more these microcosmic worlds, each with its own individual and equally captivating history, way of life and places of interest.

These islands are indeed an extraordinary archipelago, a genuine crown of pearls around the Cotentin coastline, so near but yet so far.

So near because of their proximity and the historical links associating the Cotentin inhabitants with those from the islands, or at least those not deserted, since the dawn of time and before the birth of Normandy, and even before « y-eu eun baté, portaunt ground d'touele » (there was once a ship with a large sail) and before « l'Aunglléterre fit de nout'Duc eun counquérant » (England transformed our Duke into a conqueror), as the patois-speaking poet Cotis-Capel so eloquently wrote.

So far because of the frequently conflicting interests, the fratricidal wars over the centuries and the present-day way of life, essentially British inspired for the largest of these islands which are now, and for always separated from France.

According to tradition, and even to legend, it was in the year 709 that the spring tides after the equinox, heightened by fierce north westerly winds, separated these granite plateaus from the Continent. Nevertheless, the desire for historical precision brings us to point out that this geological phenomenon actually took place 6,000 to 7,000 years before our era!

After this physical and geological detachment, a very long time after, came the political division for most of the islands to the west of the Cotentin. With William the Conqueror, the islands, an integral part of the Dukedom of Normandy, were to link their fate with the new Crown of England, whilst remaining for a long time, though in vain, coveted by France.

All of these Norman isles could well have constituted as many advanced bastions for the Cotentin mole, had they not, at this period, acquired their autonomy. This was the case, to the west, for four of the islands: Alderney, Guernsey, Sark and Jersey. As early as 1206, these islands, freshly under the control of the English Crown, were nevertheless to preserve their own laws, their legislation and their Norman institutions. The Norman lords from the two principal islands, Guernsey and Jersey, who had far more possessions on the Continent than within the islands or in England, were faced with a difficult choice. Most of them swore allegiance to Philip Augustus, in the knowledge that they would consequently lose their island goods for them to be redistributed among the Duke and King of England's partisans. The others, often less titled, chose to remain faithful to their legitimate duke, hence drawing the islands inexorably into the English orbit. Alderney, Guernsey and Sark were to find themselves grouped together within the Bailiwick of Guernsey, whereas Jersey, a different Bailiwick, was also to extend its sovereignty as far as the rocky plateaus of the Minquiers and the Ecrehou islands[1].

The only isles to remain French, although bitterly fought over with England, were Chausey, Tombelaine and the Mont Saint-Michel. The same applied, to the east of the Cotentin, for the tiny island of Tatihou, close to the shores, and to the two deserted Saint-Marcouf islands, unique within the Seine Bay, but nevertheless English for 8 years, in the early the 19th Century. Finally, in Cherbourg on the north coast, the rock known as Pelee Island served as a base for the fortifications undertaken during the last decades of the 18th Century to protect the natural harbour and the large future naval port.

So, these small maritime worlds have a rich and eventful history, astonishing institutions and a hint of mystery, all gradually unfolding throughout my different rambles from island to islet, from inhabited to deserted, almost like an initiatory quest to unveil their singular identity. I invite you, in turn, to discover a few of the men who have, over the centuries, left their mark on these tiny specks, these miniature cosmoses scattered across the English Channel. A also invite you to set foot on their shores, be they arid or hospitable, homes to simple havens or to major ports, high cliffs, heaths and moorland, modest fishermen's huts, villages or even a few towns and a great number of fortresses, collectively forming a Norman archipelago boasting landscapes which are as sumptuous as they are diverse.

(1) For more on the history of France's loss of the islands, recent work by Judith Everard from Cambridge University offers excellent further reading (refer to bibliography).

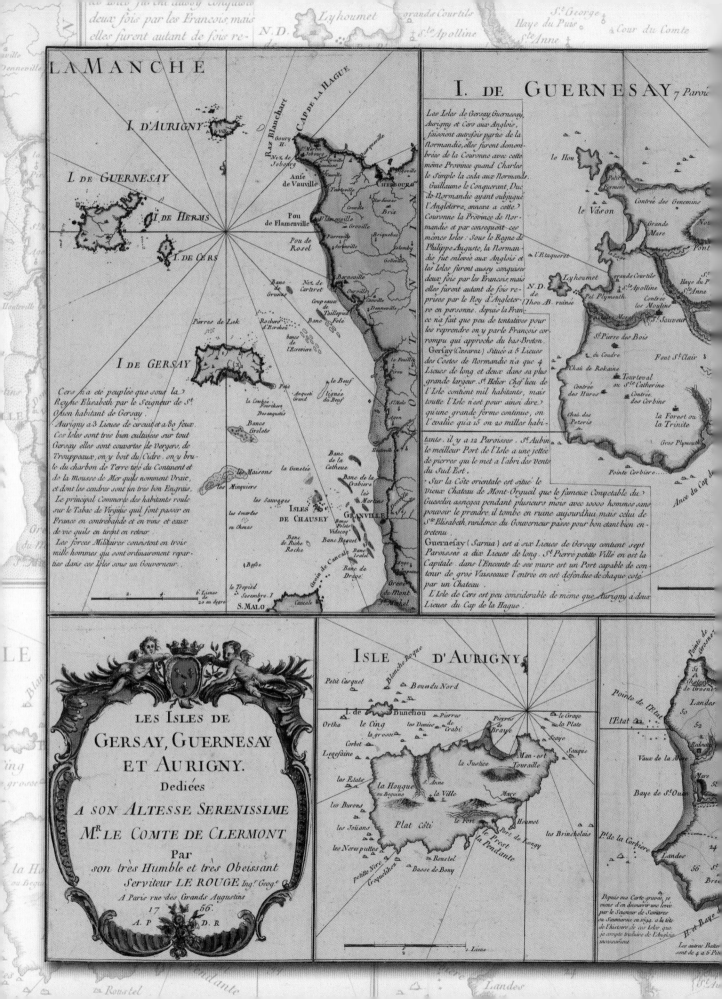

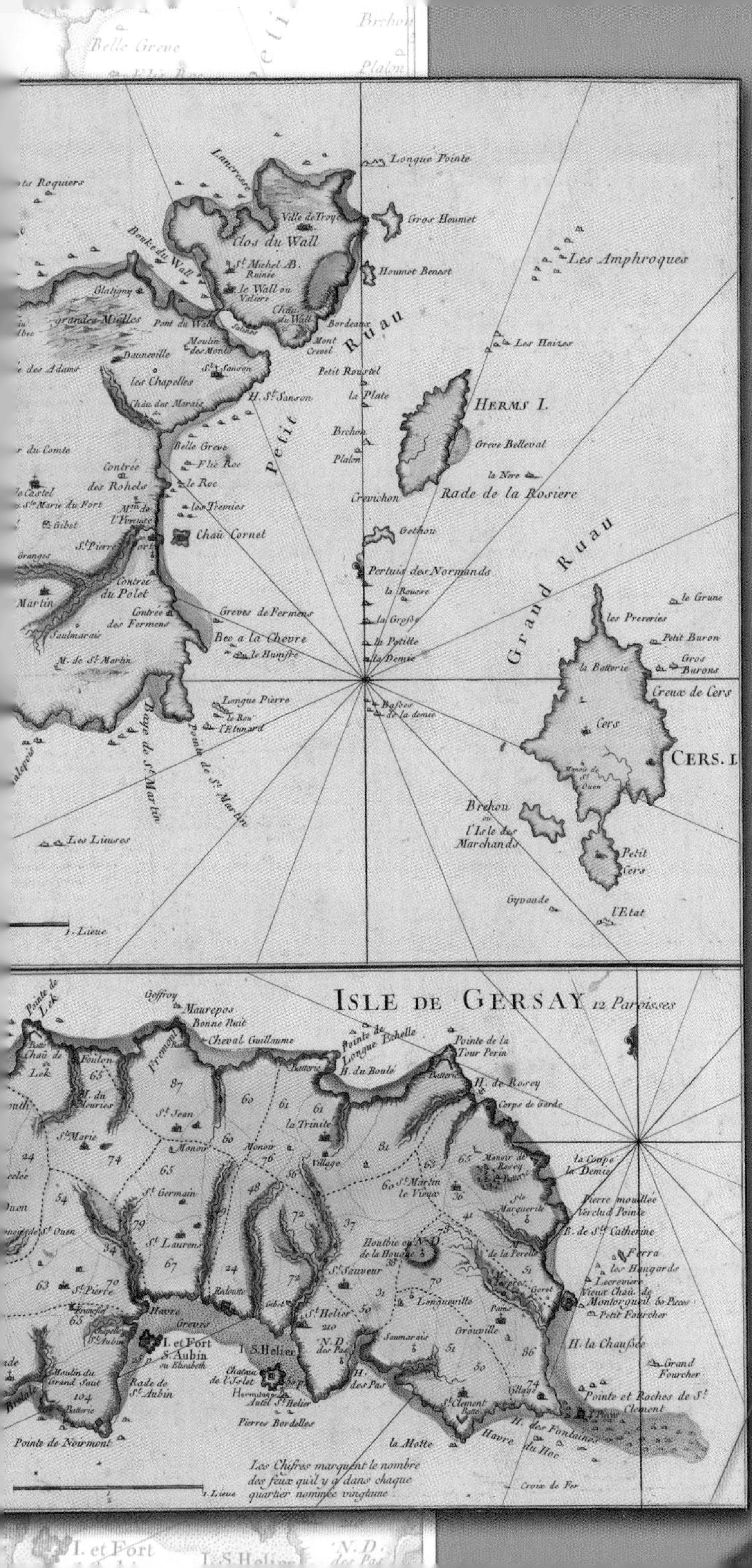

This map by the geographer Le Rouge dates from 1756, the year that the Seven Years' War began. It offers an insight into the islands' activities at the time, not forgetting smuggling! It should be noted that the text is erroneous as to the number of parishes comprising Guernsey and that Brecqhou is incorrectly located.

Thirteen years later, Lieutenant Reade arrived in Cornet Castle in Guernsey, posted in the Disabled Corps. Reade, who had been promoted to the grade of Lieutenant as early as 1755, was to fulfil a total of 32 years' military service, from 1749 to 1781. Over and above the English garrisons posted on the island, Guernsey, just like Jersey, also had a Militia, which proved to be particularly effective as from the late 18th Century.

Map labels (northern sheet):

Roquiers · Longue Pointe · Ville de Troye · Gros Houmet · Clos du Wall · St. Michel B. Ruinee · Houmet Benest · Les Amphroques · Boules du Wall · le Wall ou Valiere · Chau du Wall · Glatigny · Bordeaux · Grandes Mielles · Pont du Wall · Mont Crevel · Moulin des Monts · Les Haizes · Dauneville · St. Sanson · Petit Roustel · les Chapelles · Chau des Marais · H. St. Sanson · la Plate · HERMS I. · Belle Greve · Brehon · F'lié Roc · le Roc · Platon · Greve Belleval · Contrée des Rohels · les Tremies · Grevichon · la Nere · Rade de la Rosiere · le Castel · Mme. de l'Yvreuse · Ste. Marie du Fort · Gibet · Chau Cornet · Gethou · St. Pierre Port · Pertuis des Normands · les Preveries · le Grune · Oranges · la Rousse · Petit Buron · Contrée du Polet · Greves de Fermens · la Grosse · Gros Burons · Martin · Contrée des Fermens · Bec a la Chevre · la Petite · la Batterie · Saulmarais · le Humfre · la Demie · Creux de Cers · M. de St. Martin · Cers · Longue Pierre · CERS. I. · Baye de St. Martin · Le Rou ou l'Etunard · Basses de la demie · Pointe de St. Martin · Brehou ou l'Is le des Marchands · Manoir de St. Ouen · Les Lieues · Petit Cers · Gyvaude · l'Etat · Grand Ruau · Petit Ruau · 1 Lieue

Map labels (southern sheet — Isle de Gersay):

ISLE DE GERSAY 12 Paroisses · Pointe de Lek · Geffroy · Maurepos · Bonne Nuit · Cheval Guillaume · Pointe de Longue Echelle · Pointe de la Tour Perin · Chau de Lek · Froumon · Foulon · 65 · Batterie · H. du Boule · Batterie · H. de Rosey · M. du Mouries · 87 · 60 · 61 · 61 · Corps de Garde · St. Jean · la Trinite · St. Marie · 60 · Monou · Monou · Village · 31 · Manoir de Rosey · la Coupe · 24 · 74 · 65 · 76 · 63 · 65 · St. Martin le Vieux · la Demie · St. Germain · 48 · 56 · 60 · 36 · Pierre mouillée Verclud Pointe · Ouen · 54 · 79 · 72 · 37 · Ste. Marguerite · B. de Ste. Catherine · St. Ouen · St. Laurens · 67 · 24 · Houtbie ou N.D. de la Houque · de la Ferelle · Ferra · les Hougards · St. Pierre · 34 · Redoutte · 72 · 38 · St. Sauveur · Leereviere · Vieux Chau. de Montorgueil 80 Pieces · Francfief · Gibet · 31 · 70 · Margot · Goret · Petit Fourcher · Havre Greves · 65 · Chapelle St. Aubin · 50 · Longueville · Paint · 50 · H. la Chaussée · I. et Fort St. Aubin ou Elizabeth · I. S. Helier · 210 · N.D. des Pas · Grouville · 36 · Grand Fourcher · Rade de St. Aubin · Chateau de l'Islet · 51 · 50 · Village · Pointe et Roches de St. Clement · Moulin du Grand Saut · 104 · Hermitage Autel St. Helier · H. des Pas · St. Clement · 74 · Batterie · Pierres Bordelles · Saumarais · H. des Fontaines · Pointe de Noirmont · la Motte · Havre du Hoc · Croix de Fer · Les Chifres marquent le nombre des feux qu'il y a dans chaque quartier nommée vingtaine · 1 Lieue

Mont Orgueil Castle
in Jersey.

Contents

Alderney, in the heart of the Raz Blanchard — 12-15
Ancient times — 16-17
An island in quest for autonomy — 18-20
Alderney, the English Channel's Gibraltar — 21-26
The tragic period of World War II — 27-28
The return — 29-31
Across the island — *32-37*

Guernsey, in the centre of the archipelago — 38-40
The first settlements — 41-45
Between French and English Normans — 46-49
The Civil War — 50-51
Pirates and smugglers — 52-53
The island's 18th Century fortification — 54-59
Increasing prosperity — 60-65
Saint Peter Port and the east coast — *66-69*
The parish of Saint Martin and the south coast — *70-74*
The west and north coasts — *75-77*
Herm and Jethou — *78-79*

Sark, a timeless island — 80-82
An island of monks and pirates — 83-86
The Lords' era — 87-95
The Fief Haubert institutions — 96-98
Towards the demise of Europe's last feudal state — 99
Walks in the heart of the island — *100-111*

Jersey, the southerly British isle — 112-114
Traces of life dating from Neanderthal man — 115-117
A highly coveted island — 118-122
Jersey ready for action once more — 123-126
The 19th Century and the way towards development — 127-133
St Helier and the south coast — *134-142*
Grouville Bay and the east coast — *143-145*
The north and west coasts — *146-150*
The inland countryside, a maze of small and charming routes — *151-152*
The Ecrehou and the Minquiers, bitterly fought over reefs — *153-161*

The Cotentin islands, from west to east — 162-163
The Mont Saint-Michel and Tombelaine — 164-169
Chausey, a labyrinthine archipelago — 170-174
Pelee Island, a fortress in the Cherbourg roadsted — 175-177
Tatihou, a museum island — 178-182
The Saint-Marcouf Islands, land of seagulls — 183-187

Alderney Island.

Alderney,

in the heart of the Raz Blanchard

Alderney is quite a particular island, the most northerly of the Channel Islands, caught in the heart of the formidable Raz Blanchard. Only 8 nautical miles separate Alderney from the Cotentin shores, but the distance seems doubled when facing the counter-current winds which literally transform these otherwise heavenly waters into a furious maelstrom with colossal surging waves.

Alderney, as seen from the Raz Blanchard.

The current in this area is indeed quite considerable, reaching up to ten knots during spring tides! Furthermore, any sailing enthusiast wishing to reach Alderney by sea had better ensure that these powerful reversing currents will indeed drive him in the right direction.

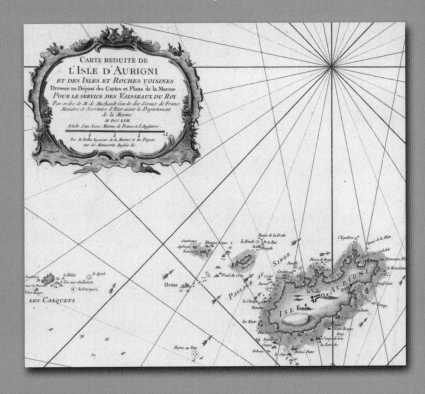

The breakwater, often covered by stunning waves.

During the winter nights, when the wind is howling like a tempest, the island is subjected to the unbridled attack of gigantic waves which come crashing onto the 800 metre long breakwater, forming strikingly high sprays of seawater, whilst, a little higher, the island plateau is swept with violent winds. There is not a copse in sight here, contrary to most of the other Channel Islands. It is difficult for any vegetation to develop. The island is wild and rugged, and that's precisely why it is so charming! It is bordered on its south coast by granite cliffs punctuated by a few rare and narrow valleys. The island's 2km large plateau slopes from the south-west to the north-east over a distance of 6km. Its north and east coasts are jagged with large bays sloping gently down to the sea, offering lovely sandy beaches separated by rocky headlands, although most of these shores are inaccessible because of the dangerous and malevolent reefs which surround them.

Many reefs surround the island.

Navigating around Alderney is difficult, particularly during bad weather, countless vessels having been dramatically wrecked in the surrounding waters.
The reefs and rock shelves surrounding the island mingle with the multiple currents, rendering the task for any navigator all the more complicated. The greater part of the north-west and the south coast is bursting with uncovered rocks, only the heads of which emerge at high tide. On the west coast, the Swinge, a narrow channel separating Alderney from the tiny island of Burhou, a chaotic mass of rocks offering refuge to a multitude of bird species, is also tricky due to violent currents, some of which cross over hitting the rocks. During spring tides, these currents can reach 8 knots, generating impressive swirls and breakers.

The Passage du Singe with the Ortac Rock (in the centre) and the Casquets to the left on the horizon.

All around the island and for a great distance westwards, the currents come against several obstacles including the Ortac Rock, and further seawards, 7 nautical miles from the port of Alderney, the Casquets. The Casquets' main island is less than 200m long.
It houses a powerful lighthouse, where all ships travelling from Ouessant to Le Havre or the North Sea came to turn before the sea traffic separation scheme pushed the navigation corridor 16 nautical miles further north-west to reduce the risk of oil slick.

So, it is not surprising that many a ship, throughout history, has been lost with both men and goods, on these perilous reefs around Alderney and the Casquets. Navigation can indeed prove to be so troublesome, be it in the waters around Alderney, Sark, Guernsey or even Jersey, that these numerous shipwrecks are an integral part of the Channel Islands' history. The highly evocative names given to the rocks which border the islands bear witness to the dangers here, such as the Noires Putes (Black Whores) to the south of Alderney, or the Paternosters, to the north-west of Jersey, to name but two!

The shipwreck of SS Stella

Among the shipwrecks etched in the collective memory, the loss of the English ferry, the *Stella*, is one of the most tragic. In the late 19th Century, two English firms offered trips to Guernsey and the Channel Islands, one of which was the London and South Western Railway Company. The permanent rivalry between these two companies had already led to incidents following dangerous manoeuvres to maintain the leading position for these cross-Channel links by offering the shortest possible crossing time.

The shipwreck of *SS Stella*, in the Casquets reefs.

On the 30th of March 1899, the *Stella* set off on her first seasonal crossing, leaving Southampton at 11.25am with 174 passengers and a crew of 43 men onboard. Although visibility was good on departure, the mist started to fall at around 3pm. The ship maintained top speed, continuing towards the Casquets instead of opting for a longer route further out to sea, which would undoubtedly have been the most prudent decision in view of the weather conditions. The *Stella*'s captain, William Reeks, despite his great experience, failed to reduce the ship's speed, simply requesting that one of his seamen look out and listen for the Casquets lighthouse foghorn.

At 3.55pm, the chief engineer informed the captain that, according to his estimations based on the number of propeller revolutions since their departure, the *Stella* must have been less than 4 miles from the Casquets rocks. Captain Reeks remained sceptical, believing that they would surely hear the Casquets' foghorn at such a short distance.

At 4pm, in a muffled growl, the *Stella* hit the Noire Roque, in the Casquets' granite reef, at a speed of over 18 knots! Although extremely violent, the shock did not bring the vessel to a halt and it continued to strike a number of other dangerous reefs. As the fog dissipated slightly, the passengers and crew could make out the rocks surrounding the ferry. The captain ordered for the *Stella* to be abandoned; however, the evacuation proved to be troublesome. The water which was gushing into the ship's hull added to the crew's difficulty in lowering the five lifeboats, one of which was overloaded and capsized as soon as it hit the water. The *Stella*'s evacuation continued but the ship sank within only 8 minutes.

Eighty-six passengers and 19 crew members perished, including the ship's captain. Tossed by the currents which drove them towards Alderney, then back towards the Casquets, the surviving passengers, loaded onto the lifeboats, were to suffer an atrocious night. Four of the lifeboats were rescued the following morning by the *Vera*, a steamship from the same company, together with the *Lynx* from its rival company.

The *Stella*, 77 metres long and with a draught of 3.7 metres, is now laid to rest on the sea bed at approximately one mile from the Casquets. Its bell is displayed in the Castle Cornet Maritime Museum in Guernsey.

Announcement of the *Stella* tragedy (as recalled by the Maritime Museum in Guernsey).

The *Stella*'s bell (visible in the Maritime Museum in Guernsey).

Ancient times

Despite this often hostile maritime environment, Alderney, which was isolated from the Continent around 7000 years BC following an increase in the sea level, has been inhabited at least since the Neolithic Age, although very few megalithic monuments have survived the island's successive fortification campaigns. In the 18th Century, the island was renowned for its many megaliths, most of which were destroyed during the construction of the new harbour and of its surrounding forts in the period from 1850 to 1860. The Druids' Altar, near Fort Tourgis, is a fortunate exception. From the Bronze Age, a few pieces of pottery remain, found in Longis Bay, the only bay facing the Cotentin coastline and the island's leading port before the creation of Bray Harbour in the 18th Century.

Longis Common is very probably, just like the more sheltered Les Marais site further inland, one of the island's very first human settle-

The Druids' Altar.

ments. Pottery artefacts from the Iron Age were discovered in 1969, during work on the golf club in the locality known as Les Hougettes (near Longis), within what would appear to be a hut destroyed by fire. The site, covered by a metre of sand and earth, had never been excavated. Grindstones dating from the Iron Age were also found in January 1999, following a winter storm on Longis beach.

Under the Roman Empire, the island was probably occupied by a garrison which built a fort, the foundations of which appear to have been unear-

thed within a building with medieval walls and resembling a fortified farm; Chateau de Longis, restored to provide shelter for the English garrison, posted on the island during the French Revolution.

Roman pottery has been found throughout the island, but essentially around Chateau de Longis, together with other Roman relics.

For a period of around 1,000 years, we have no trace of what occurred on Alderney, although the island very probably remained inhabited, contrary to Sark. The oldest reference to the island appears in a chart dating from 1042, by which William, Duke of Normandy and future Conqueror, conceded the island to the Mont Saint-Michel, before reclaiming it, only to hand it over, in 1057, to Geoffrey de Montbray, Bishop of Coutances. Following the occupation of Normandy by the French troops in the early 13th Century, Alderney, just like the other islands, was finally attached to the English Crown, but without the application of feudal tenure. This was undoubtedly due to the island's minor importance at the time, only capable of nurturing a very limited community.

The Chateau de Longis.

In 1236, a document entitled, « Status Insulae de Aurineo » illustrates that the island was already highly independent, as much from an administrative as from a legal point of view. There was a parish assembly, referred to as the Douzaine, in charge of dealing with agricultural issues, and a justice court, presided over by a provost, assisted by six jurats. The island also had a resident vicar. There were two mills on the island, one of them a windmill belonging to the

developed from its original location around Marais Square, spreading towards the present-day High Street. Longis was then the island's main harbour town, with some 700 inhabitants.

In the 16th Century, facing new threats of war, fortification campaigns were undertaken as from 1546, above Longis, on the present-day site of Essex Castle, and an English garrison was posted on the island. However, the work, deemed

cove in Cherbourg) part of the livestock taken from Alderney ».

On his return to the island on the 23rd of June, Captain Malesart invited his friends and, early July, Gouberville travelled to Alderney, by then occupied by Malesart's crew and by two further corsairs from Cherbourg, Sideville and Deneville. The best part of the day was set aside for feasting, « *faire fort grand chère* », and visiting the landing sites and the existing

Due to its location, the site where Essex Castle stands was frequently fortified. Here, the watchtower, built between 1812 and 1818 by John Le Mesurier was later transformed by the Germans.

king, and the other belonging to the bishop. The islanders, probably no more than 200 to 300 souls at the time, bred sheep and grew wheat.

When the Hundred Years' War broke out, the French captured the island in 1338, wreaking havoc. In the mid 15th Century, many immigrants from Guernsey and continental Normandy, again under English control, settled in Alderney, leading to the expansion of the village of St Anne. The town

to be far too onerous, was abandoned and the garrison left the island, henceforth defenceless. The corsair, Malesart, took advantage of this situation, plundering the site on several occasions. His first expedition, in 1558, enabled him to take livestock. Gilles de Gouberville, who knew him well, wrote the following in his diary on the 21st of June, « Captain Malesart took the island of Alderney this morning », then on the 23rd of June, in a rather festive mood, « we sold to the highest bidder in the Galé (Galley

fortifications, probably Fort Longis and those which preceded the present-day Essex Castle.

Gouberville returned to Mesnil-au-Val on Monday the 4th of July, discovering a few days later that Malesart was said to have been forced to leave Alderney by an English fleet. It did not prevent him from returning twice to pillage the island; however, his last expedition turned sour, his boat was captured and Malesart was imprisoned in the Tower of London.

An island in quest for autonomy

Douglas Quay.

Due to its increasing strategic importance, the island was conceded, by Letters patent from Queen Elisabeth in 1584, to John Chamberlain, the former governor of Guernsey's son. His ambitiousness was to be hindered by the local population, both jealous of his independence and committed to Calvinism. Alarmed by the situation, the Crown's Privy Council had the governor of Guernsey intervene, via a ruling defining the respective rights of the islanders and their Lord.

At the end of the English Civil War, Charles II granted the Island of Alderney to Sir George Carteret, chief of his partisans from Jersey, who in turn appointed Nicholas Ling as governor of the island. Whilst the island suffered economic decline, a ruling approved by the Alderney Court ordered that any children whose parents had stated being too poor to look after them were to be sent to help populate New England.

In the 17th Century, Thomas Le Cocq, a member of one of Alderney's oldest families, took over a faction reuniting a number of islanders whose desire it was to obtain total independence and to no longer be submitted to the Lord of Guernsey's authority. However, the island was to remain in the hands of the Guernseyans. After the Carterets, the Le Mesuriers governed the island for over a century, despite unrelenting opposition from the islanders.

The Government House rebuilt in 1763 (now Island Hall).

Georgian houses built near to the harbour during the 18th Century and renovated in 2005.

Henry Le Mesurier, the island's hereditary governor as from 1729, had a new harbour developed in Braye Bay in 1736, since Longis had become overwhelmed with sand. It consisted of a simple jetty, offering a somewhat unstable shelter and causing, seventy-one years later, in the winter of 1807, the loss of twenty or so boats anchored in the bay. In 1840, the jetty was enlarged and became Douglas Quay, in memory of Sir Limes Douglas, a lieutenant-governor from Guernsey.

Nevertheless, Henry Le Mesurier's harbour was to prove a precious base for the archipelago's corsairs when the Seven Years' War broke out in 1756. It offered John Le Mesurier, Henry's brother to whom he conceded his rights, the opportunity to arm privateering ships with islanders as crew. Several islanders were then to abandon their agricultural activities in favour of this, far more lucrative, maritime pursuit. Houses and warehouses were built near to the harbour (on the present-day Braye Road). These maritime activities, privateering and alcohol smuggling, generated huge profits, together with the exportation of the island's highly reputed cattle.

The population increased and the town grew and was transformed. In 1763, John Le Mesurier had Government House entirely rebuilt into a high and large three-floor building, today called Island Hall. The Clock Tower, built during the same period, is all that remains today of the former church. In 1770, a building was erected to house the island court which had hitherto convened in front of the church, in the open air weather permitting!

The Clock Tower, bell of the first church, near to the former state school.

Ecole Publique batie et fondée par JEAN LE MESURIER Ecuyer Gouverneur de cette Ifle A.D. 1790

The Mouriaux House.

Main entrance to the Mouriaux House.

In 1777, the governor's son, Peter Le Mesurier, had a handsome building erected, the Mouriaux House, which was to become the governors' private residence. Finally, a few years later in 1790, a state school, today home to the Alderney Museum was also built upon John Le Mesurier's initiative. In 1793, when the French Revolutionary Wars broke out, the British government sent a 300 man strong garrison to defend the island. This garrison was posted in Fort Longis, which had been adapted for this function by John Le Mesurier, soon to be referred to by the soldiers as the Nunnery, undoubtedly since they felt isolated as if in a convent.

A semaphore, the Telegraph Tower, was built on the island's south-west cliffs in order to communicate with Guernsey via Sark and to give the alert in the case of approaching enemy ships.

Alderney's prosperity was but short-lived, since, at the end of the wars against Napoleon, the English government removed the garrison, ceased to authorise corsairs and vigorously repressed smuggling. Facing this new economic and financial crisis, the Le Mesurier's hereditary government reached its demise in 1825, following the Crown's acceptance to buy back their rights on the island in exchange for a significant rent, whilst many families decided to leave.

In 1830, in an attempt to alleviate the general poverty, the Crown accepted that the majority of the royal land, with the exception of a strip of coast necessary for defensive operations, be divided among the island's remaining 52 peasant families. Henceforth, the inhabitants reverted to their traditional agricultural activities.

The Telegraph Tower.

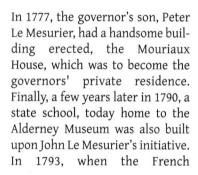

*A*lderney, the English Channel's Gibraltar

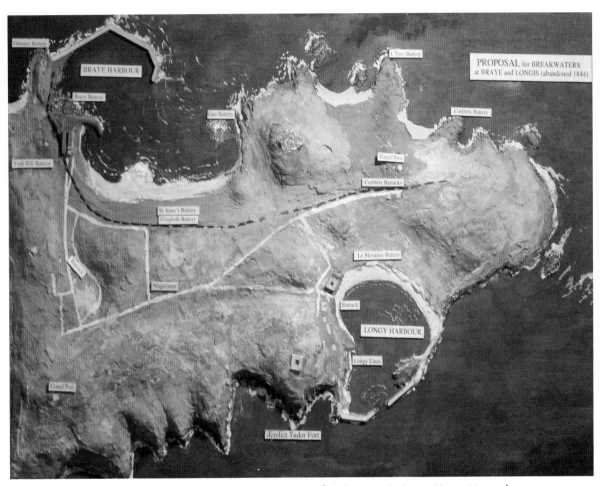

Projects to develop breakwaters at Braye and Longis (relief map on display at Alderney Museum).

Ten years later, the British government, concerned about the development of the military port in Cherbourg, decided to take advantage of Alderney's position. They planned the development and the fortification of a naval port capable of housing their war fleet. In 1844, the British Admiralty requested, from an engineer named Walker, a report on the naval bases planned in Jersey and Alderney, which was to provide a complement to the military base in Portland.

After having abandoned an initial plan to develop around Longis Bay, work finally began in Braye Bay in 1847 with the construction of a jetty to the north-west, as per Walker's instructions. The first project, which involved a port of only 27 hectares enclosed by two jetties, was already an audacious undertaking. Indeed, the most exposed of the sea walls needed to be capable of resisting the stormy westerly winds, particularly violent in these waters.

In order to protect the different buildings and barges required during construction work, a small interior port was created from 1847 to 1849, including the construction of two quays. A railway line was built from Grosnez Point, from which the new breakwater was to begin, and Mannez Quarry, in order to transport the stones mined there.

Hundreds of stonemasons, skilled tradesmen, labourers and engineers came to settle on the island to undertake this gigantic building site. Several houses were to be built in Crabby and within the vicinity of Braye Bay, in order to accommodate this working population, part of which was to remain and take root on the island. At one point, the island was even home to over thirty cabarets! A great number of brawls broke out between civilians and soldiers under the influence of alcohol.

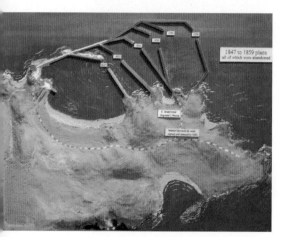

Successive projects to build sea walls between 1847 and 1859 (Alderney Museum)

The town continued to develop with the arrival of many houses and stores in Rue Grosnez (renamed Victoria Street after a visit by the queen). In 1850, the current parish church, made of Alderney granite and with a white Caen limestone facing, was built upon the initiative of Reverend John Le Mesurier, the former governor's

St Anne parish church, designed by the architect Sir George Gilbert Scott.

son, in memory of his parents. A new Court was also built in 1851 in New Street (formerly Rue des Héritiers and today Queen Elizabeth II Street), together with a twenty-eight cell prison!

On the 9th of August 1854, Queen Victoria and Prince Albert visited Alderney on the Victoria and Albert royal yacht, to inspect the sea wall and fortification work. They returned to the island in August 1857 to see how work was progressing. Over the years, the initial plan was successively reviewed to enlarge the enclosed water area, by extending the sea wall (or breakwater). In 1858, the Admiralty planned to extend the harbour's total surface area to around 60 hectares. However, work was progressing slowly, due to the far deeper seabed.

In 1864, the extremity of the sea wall was 1,463 metres from the coast. The last 548 metres had proved to be extremely difficult to build, and even more so to maintain. Following too frequent storm damage, work was finally abandoned and this part of the wall now

forms an artificial underwater reef upon which the sea often breaks. The second, initially planned, sea wall was not built.

Indeed, the site's technical construction difficulties had been underestimated. The section of the wall located the furthest out to sea would have required foundations of a depth of 39 metres under the sea bed! Deep cracks formed in the foundations during the winter months. Finally, due to the site's natural environment, the exterior side of the breakwater, which was almost vertical, produced terrifyingly high waves. Stones, 9 tonnes in weight, were projected at a height of 45 metres above the sea wall.

The port of distress, never completed, was to rapidly lose its strategic importance with the arrival of increasingly large warships and the use of steam, independently of the size of the vessel. As early as 1858, Captain Christopher Claxton had pronounced a severe judgement on what could have become the "English Channel's Gibraltar", before the port of distress

On the parish church lectern, two bibles dating from 1850, one in French, the other in English.

Fort Houmet Herbe, built around 1854, designed for an officer and 45 men and located on an islet and accessible at low tide.

One of the towers defending the inland approach to Fort Clonque.

At the foot of Fort Albert, the arsenal buildings, the command post (in beige) and the Mount Hale battery.

Fort Clonque, 1853-1855, designed for 2 officers and 50 men.

Fort Albert, 1854-1857, the largest of Alderney's forts and the only one capable of resisting serious attack.

Fort Tourgis, one of the island's largest, designed to house 32 guns with a garrison of 11 officers and 247 men.

Fort Raz, 1854, isolated at high tide and designed for 10 guns, 2 officers and 62 men.

Fort Grosnez, 1847-1852, the first Victorian fortress to be built on Alderney.

Inside Fort Grosnez in 1859 (Alderney Court collection).

selection committee. « There is not even enough space for seven vessels within the entire developed area, unless they knock into each other. They have undertaken work demanding some three thousand men to man the guns, and there are only seven hundred here ».

Simultaneously to the construction of the breakwater, fortification work was undertaken, supervised by William Jervois, a young officer from the British Royal Engineers. These forts are one of the last major developments built according to Vauban's fortification principles. Such important work was to dramatically disrupt the island's economy and its way of life. Whilst the local population was no greater than 1,200 inhabitants, this influx of several thousand English and Irish labourers led to the progressive loss of the Norman dialect, still widely used on the island in the mid 19th Century.

Only a few years after their construction, the forts, with the exception of Fort Albert which was modernised in 1900-1901, were unusable following the advent of rifled artillery.

The construction of the breakwater and the forts also resulted in the development of quarrying activities. These activities were to continue even after construction work was complete. A large jetty was built by the Admiralty parallel to the breakwater as from 1895, following bitter controversy with the islanders, unwilling to pay for such work, be it directly or indirectly. Ships could now berth at any time independently of tidal conditions, hence facilitating the exportation of the local granite and the development of tourism following Queen Victoria's visit.

The new internal jetty, parallel to the breakwater, sure to encourage port activities.

Complementary to the island's fishing and breeding activities, granite production became its primary industrial activity, employing at

forty or so farms, around 500 cattle, 40 horses and many sheep, goats and pigs. At the time, the island was governed by a local

Judge Barbenson's water pump, built in 1913 for the island's farmers.

least a fifth of the population up to 1939. Gravel is also produced on the west coast, in Platte Saline.

Ferry links became increasingly frequent with, in particular the SS Courrier, in service from 1876 to 1947.
In 1936, the Channel Islands' first official airport was opened in Alderney, transporting guests to the Grand Hotel, located at the Butes. Agriculture flourished with

government comprising a Court, States and the Douzaine. The two former institutions were presided over by the Judge. The Court dealt with civil and criminal affairs and the States, within which the lieutenant-governor of Guernsey or his representative sat, were in charge of public services, local laws and financial affairs. The Douzaine looked after parish issues.

The tragic period of World War II

Period pieces from the German forced labour camps, displayed in Alderney Museum.

Hammond Memorial erected in memory of the workers from many European countries who were deported to Alderney.

With the onset of World War II, Alderney was to experience another dramatic episode in its history. Following the invasion of France by the Germans, Alderney's inhabitants decided, on the occasion of a general assembly, to abandon the island, with the exception of a few souls. When the Royal Navy ships arrived to evacuate the island on the 23rd of June 1940, the bells of St Anne's church rang to inform the inhabitants that the departure for Weymouth was imminent. Three babies were born during this sad crossing. Livestock was transported to Guernsey and the islanders, compelled to abandon all of their worldly goods, burying or hiding the most valuable before their departure, found themselves totally impoverished upon their arrival in Great Britain.

On the 2nd of July, a few Germans landed at the airport whilst others, the great majority, arrived by sea from Cherbourg. The island was to be transformed into a genuine fortress, one of the Atlantic Wall's advanced defences, built by the Todt Organisation's forced labourers. After having appealed for voluntary workers, the Nazis used foreign prisoners as genuine slaves. In order to do so, three camps, with a capacity of around 1,500 men and one with 500 men, were created to accommodate these workers, the majority of whom under duress. The camps were named after German islands in the North Sea: Borkum (close to the road to Longis), Helgoland (near Fort Tourgis), Nordeney (inland from the Saye Bay) and Sylt (south-west of the airport).

Thousands of prisoners of different nationalities: French Jews, former Spanish Republicans, Dutch and especially Polish and Russian workers were subjected to particularly harsh conditions. The men slept on the floor in barracks devoid of tables, chairs or lights. Food was rare, mockery frequent and work was carried out at a breakneck rate, no matter what the weather conditions. Several prisoners died due to these appalling conditions, although the Nazis had not applied a systematic extermination policy in the Alderney camps. Conditions were even more severe in Sylt, the camp being run by an SS brigade. Over the years, the German garrison increased from 450 men in 1941 to 3,200 in 1943. Hitler was concerned that the British may reclaim the island, particularly after they had successfully captured the Casquets during an audacious overnight raid, despite the presence of a small German garrison.

On the night of the 2nd to the 3rd of September 1942, the Motor Torpedo Boat M.T.B. 344 with, onboard, a British commando under the orders of Major Gustavus March-Phillips, made its way to the Casquets lighthouse. The anchor was dropped 800 metres from the rocks and the assault group, comprising twelve men, boarded a small folding boat and, despite the great swell, succeeded in landing. The deafening breakers and the muffled blow of the waves, crashing into the cliff fissures, covered any noise made during the painstaking ascent of the 24 metre high rocks. After having severed the barbed wire and crossed the enclosure wall, the commando rapidly reached the courtyard, without having been located by the German garrison.
At the agreed signal from the commander, the troops rushed to their target, some of them towards the lighthouse, others to attack the wireless tower, the engine room and the troops' accommodation quarters. The surprise was total and the seven-man garrison was taken prisoner without a shot being fired.

The wireless was sabotaged with axes and the buildings searched; valuable documents were found. The commando succeeded in re-embarking at 1am, with its seven prisoners. The operation proved to be somewhat perilous due to the steep slope and the heavy swell. March-Phillips and his men regained the M.T.B 344 a little later, much to their relief. The operation, which had lasted less

than an hour, was a total success. Five nights later, another commando landed at Burhou, only to find the islets deserted.

Although much smaller than Guernsey or Jersey, Alderney was subjected to far more fortification work by the Nazis. They equipped the island with several coastal artillery batteries, the bursts of shellfire from their high calibre guns bombarding the villages

around the La Hague coastline early 1945, causing great livestock losses, damaging the Herqueville church and even injuring an inhabitant from Jobourg. The island is also home to 22 anti-air batteries and several concrete structures were built including the Mannez observation tower, the Les Mouriaux water tower and the anti-tank walls on Longis beach or at Platte Saline.

Luftwaffe listening post and water tower overlooking the town, built by the Germans around 1942 in the Les Mouriaux district.

$\mathcal{T}$he return

The flag of Alderney with the island's coat of arms in the centre of the St George's cross.

Inhabitants returning to Alderney, late 1945.

On the 16th of May 1945, the German troops occupying the island surrendered, one week after the capitulation of Guernsey. The island was in such a deplorable state that the British government did not authorise the islanders to immediately return there. Many houses had been destroyed to recuperate stone, there were several breaches in the unmaintained breakwater, land was in a state of neglect and over 30,000 mines had been planted along the coastline.

It was only in December 1945, when 300 houses had been brought back to an inhabitable state, that the exiled population could, slowly but surely, return to the island in the knowledge that nothing would be quite the same. It was decided, first and foremost, to create a community farm, aid from Britain having also been granted to rebuild houses, whilst the islanders received furniture and day-to-day goods to facilitate their return home.

Furniture provided for the islanders by the British government, on display in Alderney Museum.

The Battle of the Butes

Among the trials and tribulations awaiting the inhabitants upon their return to Alderney, one of them, an initiative by the island's chief administrator Judge French, was to leave particularly bitter memories. In order to clean the houses, the British Army had gathered together the furniture which had not been destroyed during the occupation.

Since it was difficult to identify the respective owners, the judge had the furniture grouped together at the Butes and surrounded by a rope while the islanders waited. When the rope was lowered, the inhabitants rushed to recover what they could, without possibly identifying who were the genuine owners! Referred to as « The Battle of the Butes », the affair was to generate considerable discontent, not to mention, for several decades, a few islanders reluctant to invite others into their homes for fear that they may recognise their own family belongings.

« The Battle of the Butes » (photograph on display in Alderney Museum).

The British government took advantage of this opportunity to resume insular life, for which it had granted a financial contribution, by imposing major reform in 1948 to the island's administration, through the abolition of the last remnants of its feudal system. Since the island's population was not sufficiently abundant to face the many financial costs, and given that the island's economy was to start from scratch, it was decided that certain public services, such as the police, health and education, be governed by the States of Guernsey. The Island of Alderney's budget was consequently in the hands of the Guernsey Parliament within which two Members of Parliament represented the island.

Although part of the Bailiwick of Guernsey, Alderney nevertheless has its own government, the States of Alderney, based in Island Hall and in charge of everyday affairs. It comprises a President and 10 state members, in office for a period of 4 years. The office of judge was abolished and the Court comprised a President, a function which could not be jointly fulfilled by the President of the States of Alderney, and 6 jurats appointed by the British Home Office.

Alderney's Royal Coat of Arms on the outside wall near the museum entrance.

Meeting of the States of Alderney.

However, the island kept some of its old laws and customs. One of them, which had been abandoned in Normandy, was the Clameur de Haro, still in force in Alderney in September 2003, in Sark up to May 1993, in Guernsey up to February 2000 and in Jersey up to October 2000.

This injunction enables any wronged person to appeal to the Duke Sovereign for justice to be made. The plaintiff must, on his knees and before two witnesses, call out, « Haro, Haro, Haro, come to my aid my prince, for someone does me wrong » and, remaining on his knees, he must recite the Lord's Prayer in French. The alleged wrong-doer must immediately cease the challenged activity whilst the plaintiff must then register his complaint at the Court which will then decide upon the legitimacy of his Clameur.

The origin of this appeal may well stem from the one made by the Normans to their duke Rollo, "Haro" being thought to be a contraction of, "A Rou" (Rollo).

Today, Alderney has 2,200 inhabitants and there is now only one farm producing the island's entire milk supply. The airport occupies part of the fertile Braye plateau, formerly at the heart of the island's agricultural activities. Over and above an ever-increasing tourist activity, as illustrated by the recent opening of the very luxurious Braye Beach Hotel on the site of the former and renowned Sea View Hotel, the island is now turning not only to business and offshore finance, but also to electronic commerce and internet games and gambling. Whereas the island - thankfully – has managed to preserve its charm and St Anne its picturesque cottages and old attractively coloured houses, not an office block in sight, these new activities offer an oppor-

tunity for Alderney's youth to stay on the island whilst taking on modern professional activities.

Alderney remains highly attached to its breakwater, involving extremely costly maintenance. Consequently, there was a minor revolution at the project announced in 1997 by the States of Guernsey, who finance its maintenance, to build a shorter breakwater closer to the shore, hence abandoning the maintenance of the large breakwater in order to reduce costs. The refusal was in the form of some 300 protest letters and over 1,500 signatures petitioning against the project, not only from the islanders themselves, but also from yacht clubs and individuals from Great Britain and other European countries. An independent inquiry committee, appointed by the States of Guernsey, concluded in 1998, much to the satisfaction of the islanders, that the maintenance of the existing breakwater be continued and suggested that further studies be carried out to investigate possible means of consolidating it. As one of the island's fishermen once said, « Alderney is the Breakwater ».

« Alderney is the Breakwater ».

Across the island

Mooring buoys in Braye harbour.

When arriving from the sea, visitors to Alderney discovering Braye harbour are struck by the austerity of the place: to starboard, a long sea wall which appears to barely protect from the furious waves and, in the background a daunting fortress, Fort Grosnez. On the port side, Braye Bay is more hospitable, although overlooked on the hillside by the imposing Fort Albert, but also enclosed by a superb sandy beach.
After finding a free mooring buoy – a rarity in the summer months - the sailor arriving in Alderney must then either take his tender or, if the distance between the anchorage and the quay appears somewhat daunting, rely on the dinghy shuttle service which will take him to shore.

The interior harbour and the master's office.

Sailors' tenders and, alongside the jetty, one of the high-speed catamarans providing links from the Cotentin, upon an initiative by the Manche County Council.

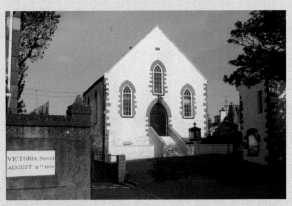

Houses in the old harbour, built opposite the 18th Century ware-houses.

Methodist Chapel, near Victoria Street.

Braye Harbour, surmounted by its small white harbour master's office, has all the charm of those harbours where all sorts of maritime activities intermingle; where fishing boats, sailing boats, small British cargo ships bringing supplies to the island or, more recently, large catamarans providing tourist links to and from France, all share the island's waterways. Multicoloured containers encumber the quays alongside a number of tenders or other small boats, each of them contributing to the overall harbour landscape.

On the way inland, the harbour leads to a narrow street lined with pubs and stores established within antique 18th Century Georgian houses and old warehouses, formerly used to store smuggled goods and those captured by Alderney's privateers.

At the top of the sheer Braye Road, forming a sort of umbilical cord between the harbour and the town, stands St Anne with its cobblestone streets, starting with Victoria Street. This is the present-day heart of the town, with its pleasantly coloured facades, its many shops, pubs and restaurants, without forgetting its banks! However, let's not stop at this, albeit extremely hospitable, thoroughfare.

Victoria Street reunites shops and restaurants alongside its colourfully painted houses.

A picturesque street leading to Connaught Square.

Le Huret.

Fort Les Houmeaux Florains.

Fort Clonque.

· Venelle Sauchet ·

A few streets have kept their French names.

The end of Victoria Street leads on to the High Street, previously called Grande Rue (before the town's expansion), which is lined with rows of interesting houses and is also home to the Clock Tower, from the former church today disappeared, and the museum. A road to the right then leads to the impressive Connaught Square where Island Hall is located. Finally, Le Huret leads to Marais Square with its old drinking trough, where the cattle market took place when Alderney was an essentially agricultural island.

On leaving the town, all roads lead to the moorland and then to the coast, since St Anne is in the very centre of the island. To the south, the high cliffs, bordered by moorland covered in gorse bush and heather, are interspersed with ravines, whilst, to the north and the west, scattered military constructions, some of them in ruins, are constant reminders of the fearsome enemy incursions set upon the islands over the centuries.

This fantastic landscape offering a medley of impressive cliffs, reefs and fortifications – of which Fort Clonque is a fine example – is a propitious setting for legends and all but a few of the islanders could tell you where the spirits favourite places were. For example, there is a rock in the shape of a chair on the beach at Clonque. A monk is said to have fought against the devil here. The holy man was victorious and, exhausted, collapsed onto the rock which was transformed into a chair to offer him comfort. The road to Clonque was haunted by a white bull and anyone encountering it was sure to meet with misfortune. At Longis, on the other side of the island, the sandstorm which raged and destroyed the former village is said to have been God's revenge against the wreckers who lived there. On the island's south side, the spirits of those who had committed suicide also haunted the Trois Vaux valley, whereas others preferred the dolmens further inland.

The Sister Rocks.

The Alderney train with its « Elizabeth » diesel engine.

Today, most of those who come to haunt the island's nooks and crannies are not phantoms but simply nature lovers looking to admire the island's fauna and flora. Alderney is home to a particular hedgehog species, Blonde Hedgehogs, discovered for the first time during the early decades of the 20th Century, together with black rabbits. Sea birds, puffins, petrels, guillemots, gulls and Northern gannets are abundant, and Les Etacs reefs, together with the islet of Burhou are genuine bird sanctuaries.

One of Alderney's other particularities is that it is the only Channel Island to still have an operational railway line. On the line built in 1847 to transport granite from the Mannez quarry to build the sea wall, the Alderney Railway Society train now runs every weekend throughout the season, much to the pleasure of its members, the islanders and, of course, tourists. Old London subway trains take you from the harbour to the quarry and the nearby Alderney lighthouse, which is open to the public. Before going on to discuss the Quesnard Point lighthouse, let's no forget the far older Casquets lighthouse.

The islet of Burhou is abundant with puffins.

Blonde Hedgehog.

At around 7 miles to the north of Alderney, the Casquets are today particularly renowned for the many shipwrecks in the "Casquets corridor", still too frequent in these waters with an exceptionally dense maritime traffic. This traffic generates over 200 radio contacts per day between the MRCC (Marine Rescue Coordination Centre) in Jobourg on the Cotentin peninsula, and the vessels travelling through the Casquets corridor.

Shipwrecks have been frequent on these reefs throughout the ages. The most famous include the HMS Victory which was torn open on the rocks in 1744, together with the aforementioned SS Stella in 1899. In 1724, following requests from the shipping companies whose vessels travelled through these perilous waters, Thomas Le Cocq, the owner of the rocks, had three lighthouses built with consent from the Corporation of Trinity House.

The three granite towers, respectively named Saint Peter, Saint Thomas and the Dungeon, were more or less equal in height and were lit by coal fires which had to be regularly kept alight with hand bellows. These towers, arranged in the shape of a triangle, were, thanks to their number, to prove easily recognisable from those located on the English or French coasts.

In 1785, the lighthouses were to be taken over by Trinity House which continuously improved their fire power. In 1877, the north-west tower was heightened and was the only one to remain lit. Seventy-five years later, the lighthouse was electrified with a range of 24 miles. Its granite tower was adorned with red and white bands. The height of the remaining two towers was reduced and a helicopter platform was added to the west tower. The lighthouse was automated in 1991 and controlled, as is Alderney lighthouse, by the Trinity House Operations Control Centre in Harwich, Essex.

At Quesnard Point, the 32 metre high Alderney lighthouse, also known as Mannez lighthouse, was built by William Baron in 1912 on the island's north-west coast, between Fort Quesnard and Fort Les Houmeaux Florains, following a disquieting series of shipwrecks on the nearby rocks, including the Liverpool in February 1902.

Its light is 37 metres above sea level and its range 23 miles. The tower is painted in white with a central black band, ensuring its daytime visibility by navigators. A foghorn, supplied by compressed air engines, was installed on the roof of the building surrounding the light-

house. Today, the foghorn is no longer in use, having been replaced by an automated system. Initially equipped with a petroleum lamp, the lighthouse was electrified in 1976 and automated in 1977.

The three Casquets lighthouses in the 19th Century.

The Casquets rocks and the present-day lighthouse.

Point Quesnard lighthouse.

St Peter Port.

Guernsey,
in the centre of the archipelago

Arriving via Great Russel, the stretch of sea separating Guernsey from the tiny island of Herm, St Peter Port welcomes you in all its splendour: a town of corsairs whose superb granite houses clutch the hillside in melodious tiers around the port, defended by the antique fortress of Castle Cornet. The maritime site is splendid and undoubtedly the most striking of the Norman archipelago.

Castle Cornet.

The view of the vast stretch of water before St Peter Port is restricted by the magnificent outline of Herm and its satellite islets, Crevichon and Jethou, with the island of Sark in the background.

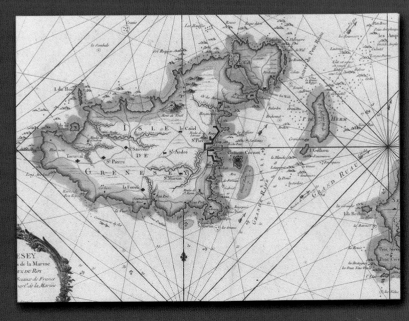

Victoria Marina, St Peter Port.

The countryside and Vazon Bay on the west coast.

Guernsey is the furthest of the Channel Islands from the French coast, at a distance of 26 miles from Carteret and located in the centre of the Norman archipelago. As such, every year Guernsey welcomes over 11,000 yachts to its picturesque harbour and is perfectly equipped to satisfy the needs of their yachtsmen. The island, which is home to 60,000 inhabitants and is divided into ten parishes, has the highest population density of all of the Channel Islands, with a total surface area of only 65km², around half the area of Jersey.

Guernsey is shaped like a rectangular triangle of a little less than 11km, the base of which comprises the south coast, bordered with cliffs. To the south of St Peter Port, which opens out onto the island's east coast, Guernsey's relief is uneven, interspersed with small valleys ending in abrupt cliffs. In contrast, the entire area to the north of the capital is flat with, on the west and north coasts, stunning deep bays bordered by a scattering of emerging rocky outcrops. Inland, there is an abundance of greenhouses specialised in growing flowers, tomatoes and fruit, often for export.

Sunrise on the island of Herm, with Castle Cornet on Guernsey in the foreground.

The first settlements

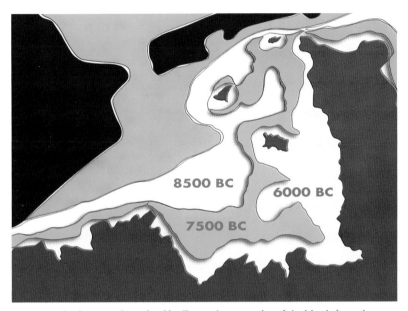

The successive increases in sea level leading to the separation of the islands from the Continent (map displayed in Jersey Museum).

Guernsey has been inhabited since ancient times, as proven by the presence of Mesolithic flint dating from 7000 years BC, unearthed at the Les Fouillages site in L'Ancress (on the island's north coast).

The island's first visitors would appear to have been Mesolithic nomads as early as 8000 years BC. These nomads hunted, looking for small game, and fished along the coast. Around 7000 years BC, a change in sea level was to isolate Guernsey from the European Continent by cutting the stretch of land which linked the island to the Cotentin peninsula, via Alderney.

The first tribes to settle on the island on a long-term basis were farmers from the Neolithic Age, between 6000 and 3000 years BC. Pottery dating back to around 4500 years BC, also found at Les Fouillages, together with stone monuments and burial mounds bear witness to their presence on the island. Sites dating from the Iron Age were discovered in 1976, including a series of circular huts with an assortment of local, rather rudimentary, pottery utensils, together with more ornate Roman style pottery. Similarly, the grave of an Iron Age warrior was unearthed in the vicinity of King's Road in St Peter Port.

One of the island's most renowned burial mounds, known as the Dehus Dolmen, although its earthen mound is perfectly preserved, is located in the Vale parish. It comprises a long chamber, 6 metres long, 4 metres wide and 2 metres high, together with four lateral chambers.

This funeral monument stands out from the island's other dolmens due to the presence of a face engraved in the stone in its interior, known as the Guardian of the Tomb. One can (quite easily) make out the face of a bearded man, armed with a bow and arrows. It is the only example of a human representation on an engraving among Western Europe's Megalithic site and very probably dates from a more recent period than the dolmen itself. On the outside, the burial mound's perimeter is consolidated with a wall of stones.

On the south-west coast, at Le Catioroc, the small Trepied dolmen comprises three blocks

Vestiges of the Les Fouillages burial mound.

The Dehus Dolmen.

standing on small stones. It was a preferred meeting place among Guernsey's witches. They celebrated their sabbaths, on moonlit Friday evenings, whilst the devil, in the form of a black goat, took seat on the dolmen and his disciples danced around him crying out in praise. Or at least, that was how the island's witches described the scene during their 17th Century trials!

The Dehus Dolmen
interior chamber.

Le Trépied Dolmen.

The Varde burial mound.

The La Varde burial mound, located at the summit of a brow in the L'Ancress moorland (to the north), is the island's largest remaining Megalithic monument. It was erected during the Neolithic Age (4000 – 2500 years BC) and was used up to the end of the Bronze Age (1000 years BC).

This 10 metre long and 3.5 metre wide tomb, together with the largest part of its six capstones, weighs approximately 10 tonnes. The site was discovered during military exercises in 1811. The Guernsey-born archaeologist, F.C. Lukis, excavated the site in 1837, to find burnt or intact human bones, abundant pottery and stone tools, bearing witness to the site's successive periods of use.

Among the island's standing stones, one of the most surprising is undeniably the statue known as La Gran-Mere du Chimquiere, next to the St Martin parish church. Approximately 1.6 metres high, this granite menhir could well be around 4,000 years old and is thought to have been sculpted during the Bronze Age, around 700 years BC, just like a similar stone in the St Marie de Castel church cemetery, symbolising the mother goddess or goddess of fertility. According to early Christian custom, these pagan places were converted and dedicated to the Virgin Mary, the Christian substitute for the goddess of fertility. The Gran-Mere du Chimquiere continues, nevertheless, to be revered by young married couples who still bring circlets of flowers to appeal to her goodwill.

La Gran-Mere du Chimquiere.

Amphorae from the Roman period, displayed at Castle Cornet Maritime Museum.

The islands were annexed to the Roman Empire around 50 years BC. Since the discovery in 1977, not far from the entrance to St Peter Port, of a few amphorae originating from Cadiz in Spain, we now know that maritime trade existed between the Mediterranean, Gaul, Great Britain and St Peter Port, during the Roman period. In 1984,

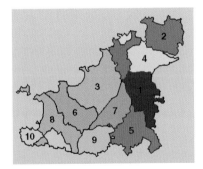

The 10 parishes of Guernsey: St-Peter-Port (1), St-Andrew (7), St-Martin (5), Forest (9), St-Peter-in-the-Wood (8), Torteval (10), St-Saviour (8), Castel (3), Vale (2), St-Sampson (4).

near the harbour entrance, the vestiges of the hull of a twenty metre long wooden Gallo-Roman boat were even found, dating back to the year 2 AD.

During the 4th and 5th Centuries, Christianity progressively spread throughout Guernsey, under the influence of the British who had come from the west of England on their way to Brittany. A little later, Welsh-born Saint Sampson landed on the island on the coast which now bears his name. The origin of the ten parishes which divide the island would appear to date at least from the 7th Century; however their history remains obscure. Each parish, with the exception of St Andrew, comprises a part of the coastline and the reason behind the territories of certain parishes, St Peter in the Wood and Torteval on one hand, and Vale and Saint Sampson on the other, being split into two distinct areas, remains a mystery. The delimitation of the parishes is possibly based on old agrarian divisions relating to primitive cultural practices. From the 7th to the 9th Century, Guernsey, just like Jersey, was part of a large Breton kingdom which even encompassed the Cotentin.

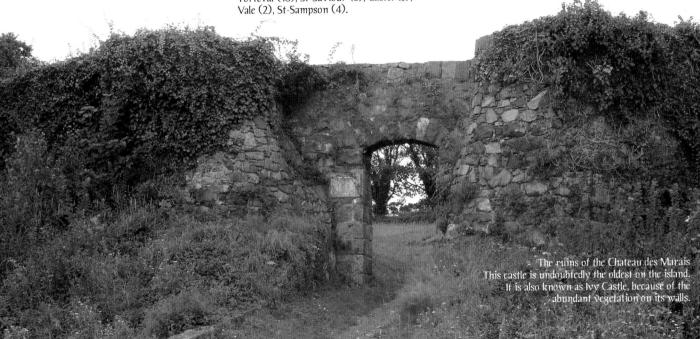

The ruins of the Chateau des Marais. This castle is undoubtedly the oldest on the island. It is also known as Ivy Castle, because of the abundant vegetation on its walls.

Between French and English Normans

With the annexation of the islands by the Normans in the 5th Century, Guernsey was to gradually adopt a new form of government; the feudal system, which is the origin of the present-day government system, although it has since been modernised. The island's laws were henceforth based on a set of feudal rules comprising the Norman Custom, in use throughout the entire dukedom.

In the Channel Islands, the first known Norman manuscripts, dating from 1022 onwards, concern donations. At the time, Duke Robert (1027-1035) was the unique owner of the island of Guernsey, together with part of Jersey. Robert then divided Guernsey into two vast fiefs which he gave to Néel of St Saviour, Viscount of Cotentin and Ranulf fitz Anhetil, Viscount of Bessin. The successive dukes, pro-

prietors of large estates in both Guernsey and Jersey, divided the remaining land into fiefs at their own discretion and distributed them among their barons and Normandy's leading religious foundations.

The Chevauchée de Saint-Michel

The Table des Pions or Fairy Ring.

Among the customs of Norman origin in force in Guernsey, the Chevauchée de Saint-Michel, although obsolete since the 19th Century, is worthy of mention. The Court of justice of St Michael, a fief covering the four parishes to the west of the island, was in charge of cleaning the railway lines to ensure that they were in a fit state for the Corpus Christi procession. Following the advent of reform, this custom was maintained in order to ensure the quality of roads, on behalf of the king.

The members of the Court and the Crown officers took part in this cavalcade, accompanied, depending on their importance, by one or two men on foot, referred to as "pions" (pawns), who followed the procession in exchange for the right to kiss the young girls they met on the way. The provosts used a very long spear, attached to a spear holder, and each obstacle they met with, such as overhanging branches, led to a fine being imposed upon its proprietor. The fines were used to pay part of the dinner which was offered on the same evening to those taking part in the cavalcade.

At the end of this very pleasant day, the pions gathered at the Pleinmont headland, on the island's western tip, to enjoy a meal seated around the vast circular "Table des Pions" (also known as the Fairy Ring), surrounded by a trench and bordered with small boundary stones, and whose origin remains a mystery.

Castle Cornet in its early days, before the keep was built, illustration displayed in the Castle Cornet Maritime Museum.

Guernsey's history was to change dramatically when John Lackland, King of England and a direct descendant of William the Conqueror, found himself dispossessed of Normandy by Philip Augustus, the King of France. The latter, on the pretence that John had neglected his vassal's obligations, undertook to confiscate the dukedom of Normandy from him by force. Hence, the greater part of Normandy became occupied.

The valiant Norman, Pierre de Préaux, who had accompanied Richard the Lionheart on his crusade in 1190 and who had been appointed Lord of the Isles by King John, was in charge of defending Rouen against the King of France's troops. After several days of siege, and having obtained no help from King John, despite his pleas, he resigned himself to surrendering the town to Philip Augustus and returned to England. The King of

France's troops then occupied the entire Norman territory.

Within the islands, Philip Augustus' supporters were initially in the majority. The convents, abbeys and priories were dependent upon Continental mother houses whereas the Norman lords, shortly beforehand, had even considered taking up arms and capturing John Lackland, who was equally despised in the islands as he was in

England. Nevertheless, the main concern among most of the seigneurial families with possessions on both banks of the English Channel was to endeavour to preserve their heritage, either by giving priority to one family member or by sharing their land among the family group.

King John was unwilling to surrender the islands due to their strategic location, ideal for an attempt at reconquering Normandy. Consequently, he set to retrieving them at all costs. It was at this point in time that the fabulous figure, Eustache the Monk emerged. His adventurous life even inspired a long and anonymous 18th Century poem!

Eustache, being the youngest child of a noble family from Boulogne, became a black monk, in other words a Benedictine monk. However, he rapidly left his abbey and, according to the legend, travelled to the Spanish town of Toledo to study magic. Upon his return, he was appointed Seneschal of the County of Boulogne, with which he became on poor terms after the confiscation of his land following his refusal to justify the integrity of his government. He declared merciless war against his lord and wreaked havoc upon the region, essentially attacking the barons' and the clergymen's possessions, whilst protecting the weak and the serfs. He then became a mercenary and a pirate establishing his bases in the Channel Islands. For over ten years, Eustache the Monk, whose audacity overwhelmed his adversaries, was to spread terror across the North Sea, the English Channel and throughout the islands of the archipelago, first on behalf of the King of England, then of the King of France.

In September 1205, the pirate monk attacked the islands with thirty galleys and took possession

of them on behalf of King John. But this did not prevent the French from launching regular raids on the isles, ravaging the harvests and copiously spreading death and destruction throughout. At the time, the loss of grain reserves was a genuine calamity for the island, life-threatening even, during the winter months, for its most humble inhabitants and occasionally forcing the lords to cancel feudal taxes. For this very reason, in the early 13th Century, Guernsey began to reinforce its defences by building a castle on an islet at the entrance to St Peter Port to ensure the island's protection. The castle was to be named Castle Cornet, after the family to whom the islet belonged.

King John, in his quest to gain the islands' loyalty, proffered the same rights and privileges upon the island's lords who agreed to swear allegiance to him as those granted before the occupation, bestowing upon them the lands lost by the Normans who had followed the King of France. However, as a safety measure, he took a few hostages among the most influential families on the islands he intended to continue to govern as Duke of Normandy. In 1254, his son Henry III conceded the Channel Islands to his own son, the future King Edward I, provided that they never be separated from the Crown of England. This particular status stands to this very day.

Losing confidence in John Lackland, Eustache the Monk left England to serve the King of France, who was delighted to secure such a fearsome and efficient ally against the English. In command of a fleet, Eustache attempted to recapture Guernsey and Jersey, occupying, with his brother(s), the Island of Sark from whence he was driven out in 1214. However, this did not prevent him

from continuing his raids within the archipelago.

Diabolical Eustache continued his acts of piracy and landed in England with Philip Augustus' troops to recruit the English barons rebelling against King John, who finally died in 1216. Following further precarious episodes, Eustache found himself, in 1217, in command of a French fleet in support of Louis, the King of France's son, who had been proclaimed King of England by the rebellious barons. However, on the 24th of August, an English fleet, faithful to John Lackland's son Henry, destroyed the French fleet near Dover. Eustache's vessel was captured and the monk was slain, decapitated. All of the towns, castles and estates occupied by Louis were given back to young Henry, including those which remained in the hands of Eustache the Monk's ruffians.

Regular raids against the islands continued throughout the 14th Century, the constant threat they posed being considered somewhat as part of the daily routine. The islands were attacked again in 1315, in 1336 and, very probably at other dates. In 1338, following an earlier raid at the beginning of the year, the French returned to devastate Guernsey in the autumn, settling there until 1340. The other islands of Jersey, Sark and Alderney found themselves under French domination and the King of France conceded the island of Guernsey to Robert Bertran, Lord of Bricquebec, whose family had owned half of the island under the reign of the Norman dukes. The French garrison remained in Castle Cornet up to 1346. On Edward III of England's request, the castle was besieged for three days by Geoffroy d'Harcourt, Lord of Saint-Sauveur-le-Vicomte, who had taken sides with the King of England. The garrison finally surrendered after violent fighting.

New attacks were organised under French impetus in 1356 and in 1372. Under the command of Owen of Wales, a renegade supporting the King of France, a powerful army landed in the parish of Castel and confronted, in murderous combat, the island's defenders who sought refuge in Vale Castle. The following year, Bertrand du Guesclin attempted to capture Gorey Castle in Jersey. In 1380, the French admiral Jean de Vienne took possession of Jersey which was to be occupied once more in 1461, for a period of seven years, by Norman captains led by Jean Carbonnel, Lord of Sourdeval, acting on behalf of Pierre de Brezé, Count of Maulévrier. At the same time, Henry VI's wife Margaret of Anjou also offered the island of Guernsey to Louis XI in recognition of his support for the Lancastrian cause. In 1468, Philippe de Carteret, helped by Vice-Admiral Richard Harliston, regained possession of the islands after having besieged Mont Orgueil Castle in Jersey for five months, and obtaining the Norman surrender.

In 1483, facing these incessant attacks which successively ruined the islands, Edward IV of England succeeded in obtaining their neutrality from Pope Sixtus IV, in the form of a Papal Bull. This neutrality was confirmed by Queen Elizabeth I when, on the 29th of July 1559, she granted Guernsey with the Great Charter reuniting all of the previously established concessions.
The islands' neutrality was respected up to 1689, when William III of England refused to acknowledge it.

Vale Castle.

From Castle Cornet, the Royalists bombarded Saint Peter Port, which was within their cannons' firing range.

The Civil War

When the Civil War broke out in England in 1642, Guernsey, contrary to Jersey, supported the English parliament. Committed to Protestantism under the influence of the French Calvinists, Guernsey's noblemen had become somewhat hostile to a king who would treat them in such a discourteous manner. Indeed, Charles I had refused to pay a ransom in exchange for the release of the crew of one of the island's ships, captured by pirates from the Barbary Coast, despite the fact that the Crown was heavily indebted to the island. Consequently, the Bailiff and the Jurats joined in the Parliament's hostility.

Still faithful to his King, the island's governor, Sir Peter Osborne, took refuge in Castle Cornet whence he bombarded the town with thousands of cannonballs, forcing the committee governing the island on behalf of the Parliament to change its meeting place. Indeed, the traditional headquarters of the States of Guernsey, referred to as La Plaiderie, where the committee traditionally met, proved to be far too exposed to royalist fire, since located at the foot of the Pollet. Sir Osborne was to resist the castle siege for eight years and nine months, although cruelly deprived of provisions, with the exception of a few supplies shipped in from Jersey.

One of the period's most famous episodes was the arrest, by the king's partisans, of three emissaries from Guernsey who had succeeded in boarding an English ship anchored in Fermain Bay, convinced that it belonged to the parliamentary camp. The ship's captain

Castle Cornet at the time of the restoration of the monarchy. The Royalist emblem can be seen above the Union flag. Painting attributed to Jacob Knyff, Castle Cornet Maritime Museum.

was in fact a royalist and he handed them over to the governor who had them thrown into a murky damp dungeon, whilst awaiting orders to execute them. However, the prisoners, who had been transferred to the high part of the Square tower located on the castle's south side, managed to escape by means of a rope woven using linen stored in the room below their cell.

Taking advantage of the low tide, together with the fact that the entire garrison was attending Sunday morning mass in the castle's chapel, the prisoners regained their freedom on the 3rd of December 1643. This spectacular escape was considered by the inhabitants of St Peter Port as an act of divine providence, in honour of which they rang the church bells with great gusto.

When Jersey gave in to the parliamentary forces on the 15th of December 1651, Castle Cornet had little choice but to surrender, in turn, on the 19th of December, with the honours of war. In May 1660 Charles II's restoration was

followed by the king's pardon, which had been claimed by several eminent families who had remained faithful to him, and Guernsey consequently preserved its ancestral rights and privileges.

During Charles II's reign, on the night of the 31st of December 1672, Castle Cornet was struck by lightning, hitting the castle's keep where gunpowder was stored. The resulting explosion was considerable, destroying the keep and the nearby buildings, including the governor's residence and the chapel, the governor escaping near death by being ejected from his bed onto the ramparts! From that date on, the island's governors ceased to use the castle as their official place of residence. Furthermore, the destroyed buildings were never rebuilt.

In 1685, the revocation of the Edict of Nantes by Louis XIV generated the mass immigration of French Protestants from France to Guernsey and Jersey, after a first influx in the 16th Century, following religious persecution in France.

$\mathcal{P}$irates and smugglers

The 17th Century heralded a period of great prosperity for Guernsey's 10,000 inhabitants, thanks to two rapidly expanding activities: privateering, following William III's repeal of the island's neutrality in 1689, then smuggling.

John Tupper, captain of the Monmouth Galley was one of the island's most famous privateers. In 1692, he informed Admiral Russel of the approach of the French fleet commanded by Vice-

Medal and gold chain offered by King William III to John Tupper and displayed in the Castle Cornet Maritime Museum.

Admiral Tourville. The latter had left Brest on his way to La Hougue, to support the landing in England of troops faithful to the Catholic King James Edward Stuart, who had been forced to leave the throne by his son-in-law William of Orange. The English fleet, together with its Dutch allies, was therefore able to take sail and to sweep down on Tourville's ships, which were far less abundant. After the first day of fighting off the Barfleur headland, the British pursued the French, burned three ships opposite Cherbourg, including the admiral's ship *Soleil Royal*, then twelve others which had taken refuge in La Hougue, on the east coast of the Cotentin peninsula.

Nicholas Thin, a qualified ship's pilot from Saint-Vaast-La-Houge, was among Tourville's seamen, recruited for Brest, in view of the 1692 campaign. So my first known ancestor already sailed the English Channel, although very probably more as a matter of duty than of pleasure!

To reward John Tupper for his initiative which had enabled the English to inflict such suffering on the French fleet, King William III offered him a medal on a gold chain. One of the sides of the

In the 18th Century, the town had many narrow streets.

medal depicts William and Mary, and the other the French ship, the *Soleil Royal* in flames.

However, it was essentially after the start of the Seven Years' War, from 1755 to 1763, then during the American colonial revolution and the Revolutionary Wars that Guernsey's corsairs were to make their fortune. In 1800, it is estimated that the capture of French and American ships earned the island the, somewhat astounding at the time, figure of one million pounds sterling! Families such as the Priaux, the Dobrccs and the Le Mesuriers, which we have also seen settled in Alderney, armed up to 35 corsair ships, many of which were built on the island, hence encouraging local shipbuilding.

Simultaneously to privateering, intensive smuggling developed in the late 18th Century, due to the extremely high customs taxes in England. This activity, which the Guernseyans preferred to refer to as « free trade », was facilitated by the island's strategic location between France and England.

The island's traders' warehouses, stores and cellars were overloaded with wines from France and Spain, and with Gin from Holland. Due to the importance of such smuggling, many factories producing easily transportable barrels and small vats were created.

Great Britain, in its efforts to counter what it considered to be illicit trading, endeavoured, several times yet in vain, to open a customs office in St Peter Port; however traders resisted ferociously, refusing the withdrawal of their traditional exemption from custom duties.

Thanks to privateering and smuggling, several of the island's families made their fortune, whereas many others lived a lavish life. These nouveau riche wished to join the sixty or so families comprising Guernsey's high society; however they were not welcomed. The resulting social dissent continued throughout the first half of the 19th Century between the « Soixantaine » and this new class of freshly wealthy inhabitants known as the « Quarantaine ».
In the 18th Century, many of the houses in St Peter Port had been hastily rebuilt after the

Civil War and the town was still essentially a network of narrow streets with neither pavements nor street lighting. Only the lower streets were paved and the waves struck the back of the houses in Grande Rue (today's High Street) and Le Pollet, the esplanade only

Town boundary, one of the stones erected in 1700 to mark the town's outer limit.

having been built during the second half of the 19th Century. However, the town had already expanded beyond the stones erected in 1700 and marking its outer boundary.

The *May Flower*, one of Guernsey's highly successful corsair ships. Scale model displayed at Castle Cornet Maritime Museum.

The island's 18th Century fortification

The considerable help offered by Guernsey and Jersey's corsairs to the British Navy was but to rekindle the French desire to capture the islands. Hence the increasingly haunting fear of French landings on the islands, leading the Guernseyans to organise an efficient militia and to fortify their coastline, essentially via the construction of small coastal defensive and observation towers linked to coastal batteries. They were later to be named the Martello Towers.

Although these towers were to be given the same name, their plans were different depending on their construction date and location, those in Guernsey being quite different from those built in Jersey during the same period. The origin of this name stems from a tower at the Mortella headland in Corsica which, during an attempted English landing in February 1794, successfully repelled several British vessels. The tower's garrison comprised only 38 men, with only one 6 pounder cannon and two 18 pounder cannons.

Guernsey's coastal defence towers

Several towers defended L'Ancress Bay.

The first towers built date from 1778, when France offered support to the Americans during the War of Independence. The British Crown granted the edification of fifteen towers, along the same lines as those also planned for Jersey. Subsequent to a deliberation by the States (the island's elected assembly), the purchase of the land required for the construction of the first three towers could not, in the case of refusal to sell, be contested via the traditional Clameur de Haro or any other form of resistance, since their edification was considered to be essential and necessary for the island's security and its defence. The other sites scheduled to receive towers were on publicly owned land. Consequently, the fifteen towers were built in a record time of seven to eight months.

Around half of the fifteen towers are concentrated along the shores of L'Ancress, in the parish of Vale, whose gently sloping bays and beaches are particularly propitious to a landing operation. The 9 metre high towers were built of granite; however they were not originally designed to house artillery, essentially providing support to the nearby coastal batteries. The low sea level due to the gently sloping shores prevented any vessel from approaching. They were consequently out of the towers' firing range.

Rousse Tower defended the entrance to Grand Havre.

Tower number 5, L'Ancress Bay.

Tower number 15, Fermain Bay. Inhabited during the 1860's by the Ferguson family, the tower also housed a tea room around 1880. A ferry service linking St Peter Port to Fermain was launched by the Mallet-Ferguson family in 1928. The tower was finally donated to the Guernsey National Trust in 2002.

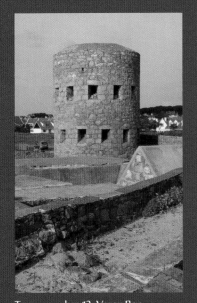

Tower number 12, Vazon Bay.

Fort Grey.

Complementary to these coastal towers, Fort George was built to the south of St Peter Port from 1780, to replace Castle Cornet as the island's strongest defensive position with artillery batteries housing, in 1801, some 135 cannons!

In 1803, Guernsey's new lieutenant-governor, Sir John Doyle, planned further reinforcements to the island's defences. Three new towers were to be built on the west coast, in Rocquaine Bay, at the Eree Bay headland and at the Houmet headland which closes Vazon Bay.

On the site of the former Rocquaine castle ruins, a semicircular redoubt was built from 1803 to house a powerful battery with a capacity of twelve to fourteen cannons and, the following year, Sir John Doyle convinced the States to build a Martello tower inside. The site was named Fort Grey and its garrison comprised an officer and thirty men.

The promontory which closes Eree Bay was used to transmit messages across the west coast via flags by day and lanterns by night. It initially only housed a simple battery, but Sir John Doyle succeeded in obtaining the construction of a tower at the battery entrance. Fort Saumarez was reused by the Germans during the Occupation. They added several bunkers and built an observation tower on the Martello tower's summit.

At the Houmet headland, where an original tower had been built, a new tower was erected within a circular enclosure. The fort was also to be reused by the Germans who built several bunkers there during the Occupation.

The Rousse Tower battery was built alongside the tower; this was quite unusual.

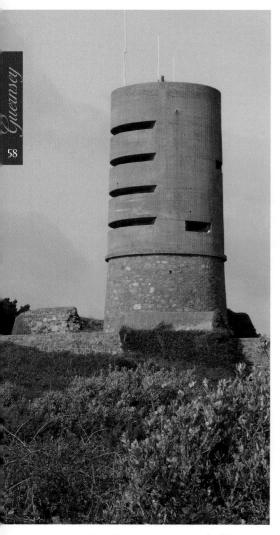

Fort Saumarez, surmounted with a
German observation tower.

Fort Houmet.

The last of the towers to be built
in the Channel Islands was not a
Martello tower but an elliptic
tower built on a rock known as
Brehon, in Little Russel, a stretch
of water running half way between Guernsey and Herm. This
fort was built with granite from
the Island of Herm, from 1854 to
1856, following the British
government's concern about the
development of the military port
of Cherbourg.

Alongside these fortification
works, Sir Doyle was also to
undertake two major projects: the
filling of the Braye du Valle and
the development of genuinely

negotiable roads. Up to 1806,
Guernsey comprised two islands
which were separated at high tide
by a narrow strait stretching from
Grand Havre on the west coast to
St Sampson's bridge on the east
coast.

Doyle believed that this arrangement would prevent him from
rapidly deploying troops onto the
tidal island of Clos du Valle in the
case of a French landing there.
The draining of the Braye du
Valle, thanks to the construction
of two sea walls enabled 120 hectares of land to be reclaimed for
cultivation and St Sampson harbour to be developed, hence facilitating its trading activities.

In 1805, these three towers, each
of which was to house a carronade, were not yet complete when
the troops posted there began to
complain of the lack of comfort
and of natural light in their quarters, together with the fact that
the rain filtered through the cannon platforms. They had been
built by negligent labourers; the
masonry was poorly executed and
was occasionally even devoid of
mortar! The Rocquaine, the largest of the towers even collapsed
as soon as the arch-shaped vault
was built.

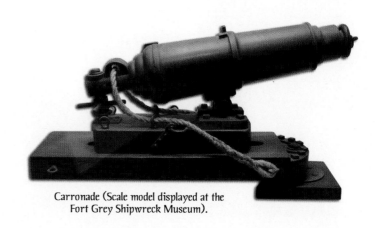

Carronade (Scale model displayed at the
Fort Grey Shipwreck Museum).

Although the local inhabitants considered the island's poor road network to be an asset, since it would present a genuine hindrance to any invader, Sir John Doyle nevertheless succeeded in convincing the States to improve it. Military Road was built, hence facilitating the transport of troops and supplies to the north of the freshly unified island, together with two further roads leading to Eree Bay and Vazon Bay. Other roads were built later, the States having realised the benefit of improved links between the rural parishes and the island's interior. The Guernsey islanders' gratitude for John Doyle's work was expressed in the form of a monument in his memory, erected at Jerbourg Point, shortly after his departure from the island in 1816. This

Fort Grey was armed in 1816 with a 24 pounder carronade on its tower, together with a further six 24 pounder cannons (Scale model displayed at the Fort Grey Shipwreck Museum).

monument was unfortunately destroyed by the Germans in 1944, to be replaced after the war by the Doyle Column.

The Doyle Column.

Before being drained, the mouth of the Braye du Valle was protected by Martello Tower N°3 (now named Mont Crevelt Tower), and its right side by Vale Castle.

Increasing prosperity

Elizabeth College.

The former meat market, built in 1822 and recently renovated, has lost its original function.

During the 19th Century, the island's population increased from 16,000 to around 40,000 inhabitants, generating considerable urban development along its main roads. Major works, accelerated by a cholera epidemic, were to modify the appearance of St Peter Port. The town's streets were enlarged and paved, a sewerage system was installed and certain houses were demolished to allow more light to pass through.

The construction of new buildings, added to Elizabeth College founded in 1563, was completed in 1829.

The Poids de la Reine.

Large town houses replaced older buildings. Indoor markets were built from 1822 to 1830, then again in 1873, whereas a small building referred to as the Poids de la Reine was built in 1876 to house the public scales.

The fish market.

Maritime transport enjoyed a newfound youth, sailing ships gradually being replaced by steamships. *Le Médina* was the first steam ship to arrive in Guernsey in 1823, launching what was to become a regular ferry service to Weymouth. The links became increasingly frequent in the summer months with an escalating rise in the number of tourists to the island, essentially wealthy and curious visitors seeking to enhance their general knowledge or nature enthusiasts keen on botany and ornithology.

Queen Victoria, in the company of Prince Albert, made her first visit to the island in 1846. The Victoria Tower was erected two years later to commemorate this inaugural royal visit; a second visit was to follow in 1859.

St Peter Port seen from Victoria Tower.

pleted Sir John Doyle's new road network.

The island's rural activities were also on the upsurge. The breeding of the renowned Guernsey cattle, imported from Normandy in the 10th Century, continued throu-

of heated greenhouses as from 1877. Most of these greenhouses were used to grow grapes, hence their name, « *vineries* ». Grapes were rapidly overtaken by tomatoes, otherwise known at the time as "apples of love" or "golden apples", their cultivation totally

Victoria Tower, designed by the architect William Bunn Collings.

A Guernsey cow.

Flowers, often intended for export, are also sold on the island.

Greenhouses with Vazon Bay in the background.

The island's mounting prosperity, enhanced by the development of naval construction and granite exports to England, rapidly rendered St Peter Port inadequate, hence its subsequent expansion. Large avenues comprising the north and south esplanades com-

ghout the 19th Century. However, the rules of inheritance in place at the time prevented breeders from enlarging their farms and, to ensure a complementary income, they opted for diversification through fishing and horticultural activities. Hence the development

replacing that of grapes after World War I. Tomatoes were to remain the island's main crop up to the 1960's, before the development of floriculture which remains to this day a prosperous activity, with over a million cases of flowers exported each year.

Victor Hugo and his family at Hauteville House.

In the mid 19th Century, Guernsey welcomed many French exiles, among whom Victor Hugo. The great poet was initially exiled to Jersey in 1852, before being deemed unwelcome for having stood up for a journalist who had criticised Queen Victoria's visit to Napoleon III. Victor Hugo arrived in Guernsey on the 31st of October 1855 and, the following year, purchased Hauteville House where he lived for fifteen years.

Hauteville House.

In a letter addressed to Octave Lacroix, he highlighted the originality of his situation, « *I live near the sea in a house built sixty years ago by an English privateer and called Hauteville House. I, a representative of the people and exiled soldier of the French Republic, pay droit de poulage every year to the Queen of England, sovereign lady of the Channel Islands, as Duchess of Normandy and my feudal suzerain. This is one of the curious results of exile!* »

Whilst pursuing his literary works, including The Toilers of the Sea, which pays tribute to the inhabitants of Guernsey, the author decorated Hauteville House with Delft pottery, Chinese curio, tapestries, antique chests, wooden panels which he sculpted himself, all intermingling in the strangest of atmospheres where the irrational and the most daring of Baroque became one.

Statue of Victor Hugo, by Jean Boucher, commemorating his exile in Guernsey. Donated to Guernsey by France on the 7th of July 1914 and erected in Candie Gardens.

The dining room at Hauteville House.

After his return to France, following the fall of the Second Empire, Victor Hugo only came back to Hauteville House three times. The house was conceded by his great grandchildren to the City of Paris in 1927. A statue by Jean Boucher was donated by France and erected in Guernsey's Candie Gardens in 1914 in commemoration of his exile on the island.

The early days of the 20th Century proved to be very peaceful for the Guernseyans. However, upon the declaration of World War I, although conscription was not in force on the island, over 7,000 of its 40,000 inhabitants volunteered to join the war efforts in France. The Royal Guernsey Light Infantry was even to suffer heavy losses in Cambrai in 1917.

English was adopted as the official language in 1921 and the French franc was abandoned as the official currency in favour of the pound sterling, which had been concurrently used over many years.

With the onset of World War II, and for the first time in its history, Guernsey was considered to be indefensible. The island was demilitarised to protect it from being devastated by German bombs. Compared to the neighbouring islands, many more of Guernsey's inhabitants had kept close contact with England or were recently immigrated; consequently, around 40% of its population left for England before the Germans arrived.

Many defensive structures were built on the island by its new occupant, often in the same locations as older fortifications, together with miles of subterranean galleries intended to provide shelter for troops and supplies. During the Occupation, the island's Bailiff, Sir Carey, endeavoured to protect the rights of his citizens. After the Allied landings in Normandy, the islands were isolated and could no longer be provided with fresh supplies. In order

One of the subterranean galleries created by the Germans.

Display depicting the transport of supplies by the cargo ship *Vega* (German Underground Hospital in Jersey).

sessions, with the right to speak but not to vote. Since 2004, the island is governed by ten ministers, all of them Members of the States of Deliberation.

The Bailiwick of Guernsey, which is not a dependency of the United Kingdom but of the British Crown, has its own postage stamps since 1969, together with its own full

Bailiwick of Guernsey postage stamps.

to save the islanders from famine, Sir Carey obtained permission from the Germans to have the Swedish cargo ship *Vega*, belonging to the Canadian Red Cross, docked in St Peter Port. On the 27th of December 1944, the cargo unloaded 750 tonnes of supplies for the two islands, making several similar deliveries over the following months. The German garrison was only to surrender the day after the Nazi capitulation, on the 9th of May 1945.

After the Liberation, the 1948 Reform Law formally distinguished

legislative and the judicial system. The States include forty-five elected members, together with two representatives from Alderney. Finally, the lieutenant-governor representing the Crown, the attorney general and the solicitor general are invited to the States

Guernsey's flag, created in 1985. This flag, bearing the St George's cross, with a superimposed golden cross, taken from William the Conqueror's own standard, has replaced the island's previous flag bearing a simple St George's cross and often confused with the English flag.

series of coins since the adoption of the decimal system in 1971. The British government remains in charge of the island's defence and its foreign relations; however the Bailiwick is consulted, as is Jersey, before any international agreement with a potential impact on the island is concluded. Such was the case with regard to the Treaties of the European Union, of which the Channel Islands are not members, having succeeded in negotiating a status enabling them to preserve their insular particularities such as their tax and trade independence.

The Royal Court.

Poster celebrating the Liberation, displayed at the Guernsey Museum.

judicial power from legislative power, whilst maintaining the Bailiff at the head of the States of Deliberation and President of the Royal Court. However, the 1948 law prohibited the Jurats from sitting on the States in order to avoid cumulated functions within the

Lloyds Bank, St Peter Port.

Today, despite the absence of raw materials or processing plants, Guernsey's economy is booming thanks to its particular tax status, and is taking on an increasingly British appearance. The island's old and original Norman foundations are gradually and inevitably being erased in favour of English culture. Since the 1980's, concurrently to horticulture and tourism, international banking has blossomed, thanks to the presence of a number of major world banks in Guernsey, together with many insurance companies or investment funds. The island is now facing overpopulation which needs to be kept under control, if Guernsey's enchanting living environment, until now successfully preserved, is to be maintained. This environment is also the source of a precious tourism potential, rendering the island a particularly attractive destination.

St George's Esplanade has preserved a very traditional character.

To the north of St Peter Port, Admiral Park reunites modern residential and business accommodation.

Saint Peter Port and the east coast

Houses clutching to the hillside.

The parish church of St Peter.

Visitors arriving at Guernsey by sea are immediately charmed by the graceful layout of St Peter Port, with its houses overlying in tiers from the shore to the hills all around the harbour. And when they set foot on Guernsey soil, the charm is no less engaging. This maritime city is characterful not only thanks to its narrow streets, often winding and abundant with boutiques, but also its steep pathways, lanes and steps ascending as if towards infinity from the harbour to the town heights.

St Peter Port made its fortune thanks to its corsairs and smugglers, and the town has preserved a unique atmosphere from those bygone days, to be found nowhere else. Take a pleasant stroll and discover the town's different districts, its picturesque houses, attractive old markets, its church, the Royal Court, its gardens and museums, including the remarkable Guernsey Museum and Art Gallery located within

The parish church altar.

the Candie Gardens with splendid views of the harbour. And finally, for Victor Hugo enthusiasts, Hauteville House is a must!

High Street, one of the main shopping areas.

18th Century houses near the seafront.

The Constitution Steps, St Peter Port.

Castle Cornet

Other very interesting museums, starting with the Maritime Museum, are located within Castle Cornet which, as a fortress, is itself well worthy of a visit. Up to the late 18th Century, the castle remained the showpiece among the island's fortifications, before the construction of Fort George to the south of the town. The latter, purchased by the States in 1958, was then resold to an English property development company which built luxury apartments on the site. Castle Cornet was also used as a prison up to 1811 and, throughout the 19th Century, part of the English garrison remained posted there. Then the Germans took over the fort in 1940.

When leaving St Peter Port on the way to St Sampson, the island's second harbour, visitors are surprised to discover, facing this charming site with Little Russel

and the islands of Herm and Jethou in the background, the ultramodern Admiral Park development. Albeit of doubtless architectural quality, the development is a clear break from the old corsair town, comprising contemporary grey aluminium and glass constructions, housing residential and business accommodation, together with retail outlets.

An 18th Century Castle Cornet garrison bedroom.

The Saluting Battery, Castle Cornet.

St Sampson.

Castle Vale ramparts and entrance.

Thousands of tonnes of granite were exported from St Sampson during the 18th Century and, today, the town is a highly active commercial port importing heavy goods. With its small colourful houses, its many shops and a vast range of businesses, St Sampson embraces a typically industrial atmosphere, accentuated by the presence of cranes, huge storage tanks, smoking factory chimneys and a power station. As the island's second largest town, St Sampson, which is home to many of the banks and businesses established in Guernsey, remains an extremely lively destination where the pubs are renowned.

When leaving St Sampson continuing northwards along the coastline, on the heights stands Vale Castle, initially intended to protect from approaching vessels in the Braye du Valle strait which separated Guernsey from the north of the island. The site is in fact a very old Iron Age fort comprising a large mound of earth protected by a ditch. The stonework enclosure visible today dates essentially from the 16th and 17th Centuries; however the entrance, the site's oldest part, dates back to the 15th Century.

Recent archaeological excavation work unfortunately failed to unearth the vestiges of the medieval castle. Vale Castle is in fact older than Castle Cornet, its early construction having begun as early as the 12th Century.

In 1372, the castle provided shelter for the inhabitants of the Clos du Valle (which, at the time, was separated from Guernsey) when Owen of Wales wreaked havoc upon the island and, after having besieged Castle Cornet, came to Vale Castle to do likewise, before returning home with ill-gotten money and jewellery. In the 18th Century, new barracks and officers' quarters were built and the castle was rearmed, whilst France formed allegiance with the American colonies during the War of Independence.
Its weapons were to remain in place during the French Revolutionary and Napoleonic Wars.

During the Occupation, the Germans demolished the abandoned barracks and modernised the fortifications, installing mortar and various guns, trenches and bunkers.

Little Russel seen from Bordeaux Harbour.

The parish of Saint Martin and the south coast

To the south of St Peter Port, the parish of St Martin boasts wild landscapes and pleasant walking routes across the woodlands and shaded valleys. Its steep coastline and its creeks are particularly characterful. Renoir, who spent six months painting and drawing in Guernsey in 1874, was particularly inspired by the Moulin Huet Bay.

Closer to St Peter Port, the Fermain Bay creek is far from devoid of charm, with its pebbled beach nestling in the verdant landscape, its Martello tower on the heights and its small sentry box, referred to as the Pepper Pot.

Immediately inland, in the heart of an impressive estate masked by a curtain of verdure, stands Sausmarez Manor. This superb manor house, open to the public, has been the propriety of the Sausmarez family for eight centuries.

The first traces found in Guernsey of the Sausmarez family, of Norman origin and from the fief of Samarès in Jersey, date back to 1115. The fief and the manor remained the family's propriety up to 1557. At the

Sausmarez Manor.

time, the lord, Georges de Sausmarez, died without heirs, leaving the estate to his sister, whose husband, John Andrews, was an English officer from Northamptonshire. Their son, known as John Andros, due to the mispronunciation of his name by the locals who spoke "Guernsey French", had the second manor built in 1585.

The magnificent Moulin Huet Bay.

In 1674, Sir Edmond Andros, Bailiff and lieutenant-governor of Guernsey and, simultaneously, governor of the colony of New York, together with other American colonies, had plans drawn for a dwelling more in keeping with his social status. However, it was his nephew, who inherited the estate, who finally had the transformation described in his uncle's testament completed. Hence, an elegant manor in Queen Anne style was built of red and grey granite from 1714 to 1718. At the very top of the roof, a balcony was used as an observatory for the wives of sailors awaiting the return of their husbands vessels.

John's nephew, Charles Andros, the new lord as from 1746, sold the manor and the fief back to the Sausmarez family who owed its newfound wealth to privateering, hence recovering its ancestral heritage to hold onto it to the present day. The manor has, however, undertaken many renovations to suit the needs and the desires of its successive inhabitants.

St Martin's church.

Bronze plaque commemorating James
Saumarez' great feat in 1794.

Lord Admiral Saumarez (who dropped the second "s" when he enlisted) was among the Sausmarez who served in the Royal Navy, together with Captain Philip Sausmarez who left part of his fortune to his brother John to help him buy back the manor in 1748. James Saumarez, commander of a small squadron of three frigates in 1794, was confronted with five French frigates and succeeded, with the help of an experienced pilot, in returning to Guernsey's west coast, readily braving a narrow labyrinth of rocky waters, forcing the French to abandon their pursuit and a virtually guaranteed victory. A year earlier,

Saumarez had come to the Normandy coast by night, to bombard the harbour and the town of Granville, in an attempt to destroy one of the construction sites where Bonaparte's First Consul was preparing a fleet for the forthcoming English invasion.

The parish of St Martin is also home to a lovely 18th Century church near the Gran-mere du Chimquiere, which replaced a former wooden construction built on the site of a mausoleum from the Neolithic Age. Its more recent south porch is undoubtedly the island's finest example of Flamboyant Gothic architecture. In 1048, the parish of St Martin was conceded by Duke William to the Abbot of Marmoutiers, at the same time as he conceded a further five of the island's parishes.

Gothic porch at St Martin's church.

The Little Chapel, built by Brother Déodat.

In the parish of St Andrew, the German underground military hospital, built during World War II and similar to its Jersey counterpart, is a maze of tunnels hollowed out by forced labourers, deported from across Europe, intended to shelter German bombs and equipment. Not far from there, in Les Vauxbelets, stands a decidedly more peaceful building, on the slopes of a wooded hillside; the Little Chapel. Built between 1914 and 1923 by brother Déodat, one of the Brothers of the Christian Schools, founded by Jean-Baptiste de la Salle, this relatively uninviting chapel is at the very least original, adorned with shells, pebbles and coloured pieces of porcelain and has a nearby grotto similar to the Notre Dame grotto in Lourdes.

Travelling towards the coast via the Pleinmont road, visitors are sure to notice the curious St Philip church spire in the parish of Torteval.

Pleinmont Point, extensively armed by the Germans during the Occupation, offers a superb panoramic viewpoint, from which the Hanois Lighthouse can be admired rising from a reef, on the furthest west of the rocks emerging 2km from the island's shores.

The Hanois Lighthouse.

Torteval church.

German observation tower erected on Pleinmont Point.

One of the Generaloberst Dollman battery guns, which was operational as early as December 1941.

Subsequent to Hitler's 1941 directives ordering that the Channel Islands be transformed into naval fortresses, the Germans realised that the Navy alone could not fulfil such a mission and decided to fortify the coastline. To ensure the defence of Guernsey's south and west coasts, they erected coastal artillery batteries on Pleinmont Point, together with a five floor observation and firing command tower.

The gun which was housed in the Generaloberst Dollman coastal artillery battery was restored on site in 2001, as a testimony to the armament set up by the occupants. The Generaloberst Dollman battery inclu-

ded four 22cm guns with a firing range of 22km (14 miles). These guns had been built for the French army by Schneider during World War I, to be transported to the island by the Germans following the French invasion in 1940.

Along the coast, a pedestrian walkway meanders across the moorland leading to the foot of the cliff where walkers can discover the *Table des Pions* (Fairy Ring) and the very old Fort Pezeries, built on the rocky outcrop and altered during the Napoleonic Wars.

Fort Pezerie.

The west and north coasts

The west coast, with its many bays, is well worth a linger. Fort Grey, in the parish of St Pierre du Bois (St Peter in the Woods), was built from 1803 to 1804, occupying a small peninsula close to the shoreline in Rocquaine Bay, formerly notorious as a place where witches gathered for their sabbaths. Fort Grey's very interesting Maritime Museum, located within one of the island's large Martello towers, depicts the shipwrecks and the many seafaring tragedies having occurred in the waters around Guernsey.

To the north, Rocquaine Bay is followed by Eree Bay, both being closed by a small headland upon which stands Fort Saumarez, defaced by the addition of a German observation tower. In front of this small headland, the island of Lihou, which can be accessed on foot at low tide, was once home to an important 10th to 14th Century Benedictine priory.

Vestiges of the shipwrecked *HMS Sprightly*. This cutter, lost in the Hanois reef in 1777, was discovered by the Belgian diver Robert Stenuit in 1973.

Top-left insert: Modillion in Caen limestone from the Lihou priory and dating from the late 13th Century (on display at the Guernsey Museum). Background picture: Lihou which can be reached via a paved causeway at low tide.

The site where the Mont Chinchon battery stood.

Moving further inland towards La Grande Rue, visitors then discover St Apolline's chapel, a delightful example of perfect restoration among the many of the religious buildings which stood on the island during the 14th Century. Along the coast, Vazon Bay offers fine sandy beaches where Guernsey's surfers enjoy daring its breakers. At the Albecq headland, stands Fort Houmet, in turn converted by the Germans. The road then opens out onto the magnificent Cobo Bay with its pink granite, whereas the Route de Cobo which leads to St Peter Port passes near Saumarez Park and its Folk Museum.

In the parish of St Saviour, next to Le Trepied dolmen, the ruins of the old Mont Chinchon battery are still visible. This battery was armed with two 20 pounder cannons, aimed at preventing the French from landing to the south-west of Perelle Bay.

Chapel devoted to St Apolline, an Alexandrian martyr invoked against toothache.

Back on the coastal road northwards, the Grand Havre, a deep coastal indentation can be reached. Before 1806, this bay extended inland to join the St Sampson gulf, transforming, as we have already mentioned, the greater part of the parish of Vale, referred to as the Clos du Valle, into a separate island.

L'Ancresse Road runs alongside Guernsey's superb golf course, boasting a number of Megalithic sites and Martello towers dating back to the Napoleonic period. L'Ancress Bay is one of the island's most beautiful bays offering a vast and sandy beach. After the two north-east headlands, respectively defended by Fort Le Marchant and Fort Doyle, built around the mid 19th Century, visitors then discover Beaucette Marina, developed from a former granite quarry which was connected to the sea. Finally, via La Rochelle Road, the fascinating Dehus Dolmen is well worth a visit.

Vale church.

L'Ancress Bay.

Herm and Jethou

Herm's tiny harbour and its surroundings are frequently visited by Guernseyans who come to spend a few hours on the island or for a drink in one of its pubs.

Herm offers a variety of landscapes.

Jethou and Crevichon seen from Herm, with Guernsey in the background.

Opposite Guernsey's east coast, the islets of Herm, Crevichon and Jethou delimit Little Russel, 4 miles of strong currents scattered with rocks which emerge at low tide, thus rendering access to Herm particularly troublesome. Although at high tide, after having scrupulously respected the passage drawn by the Alligande, Godfrey and Vermerette beacons, the tiny harbour built in the early 19th Century to transport granite can be reached by sea, the same cannot be said at low tide. The alternative route involves sailing to and berthing at the Rosiere Steps, via the Percee Passage.

Herm is less than 3 miles from St Peter Port. This small island measures a mere 800m large and 2.2km long. Its proportions, together with its peaceful and serene landscapes are reminiscent of those mysterious treasure islands that enchanted our childhood fantasies.

The south is relatively high, with areas of 60 to 70 metres, and the island is covered with woodland and pastures where the cows graze, gradually descending towards sea level to the north. Herm boasts superb dunes and fine sandy beaches such as Schell Beach on the east coast, deserted and reminiscent of the very first dawn. The village's few houses are clustered together around the harbour on the west coast. Its sixty or so inhabitants share this tiny haven where nature is totally preserved and travel is by foot.

Herm has been the property of the States of Guernsey since 1946, and is rented to Adrian and Pennie Heyworth. Pennie is Major Peter Wood's daughter, her father having obtained a 100-year lease in 1949. Following painstaking efforts to restore the island, which had been left to abandon during the post-war years, Peter Wood has transformed Herm into a haven of peace, sheltered from the contamination of the outside world, whilst nevertheless opening its shores to tourism.

The neighbouring islands of Jethou, Crevichon and Grande Fauconniere, to the south of Herm, are private estates and landing is strictly prohibited.

Schell Beach in Herm.

Ferry arriving at the
Maseline Bay jetty.

Sark,

a timeless island

Close to Guernsey, Sark is, together with Alderney, one of the wildest of the Channel Islands and is also the most difficult to reach, surrounded by a multitude of rocky reefs which need to be threaded through in order to reach Maseline Bay quay or the tiny Creux Harbour nearby, only capable of welcoming small fishing boats or a few yachts.

The Buron Rocks and the Maseline Bay jetty. The passage between these islands offers a depth of barely 1 metre at low spring tide.

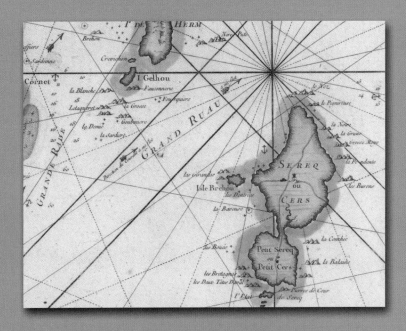

Built in 1588 by Philippe de Carteret, then renovated in 1860 by the Reverend W.T. Collings, Creux Harbour is unsuitable for today's maritime traffic. Shipping companies therefore always berth alongside the quay in Maseline Bay. This short jetty has served as the island's port since 1949. It is the place where visitors and goods gather, where exchange with the outside world takes place; an outside world which is, even today, only accessible by sea.

Similarly to Creux Harbour, at the jetty's extremity, a tunnel has been hollowed out in the cliff side to provide access to the island.
A steep yet tarred pathway, the only one on the island, offers access to the summit of the plateau. Indeed, the island of Sark, 5.5km long and barely 2km wide, is a high granite plateau dominating the sea on all coasts, frequently from an altitude of 100m above sea level.

Sark comprises two quite distinct parts, Great Sark to the north and Little Sark to the south, linked by an extremely narrow isthmus, called La Coupee, large enough only for small carts to cross it and bordered by breathtaking precipices.

To date, Sark's 600 inhabitants have succeeded in preserving the island from the often superficial or secondary values attached to modernity, by maintaining a wise way of life and an exceptional living environment. A stone's throw from the verdant pastures and prairies, wooded valleys lead to the sea, to the island's 60kms of coastline and its many grottos hollowed within its high cliffs.

The very picturesque Creux Harbour is totally dry at low tide.

An island of monks and pirates

Dolmen on the Rouge Terrier heights.

Just like all of the islands in the English Channel, Sark was inhabited during the Bronze Age; however, rare are its prehistoric vestiges. The existence of ten dolmens was recorded in 1874; however they have almost all been destroyed for their stones to be recovered. Two remain, nevertheless, visible to this day, one of them located on Little Sark, on the Rouge Terrier heights. A bronze dating from the 5th Century, discovered during the 20th Century, bears witness to a Gallic settlement on the island. Very recent archaeological excavation, undertaken in July 2006 by Professor Sir Barry Cunliffe and his team from Oxford University, unearthed pieces from both the Gallic and the Roman periods.

It was only during the 7th Century that the first mention of the island was made in the chronicles when St Magloire founded a monastery within a wooded valley on the site of the present-day Seigneurie. The island's toponymy has preserved the memory of this monastery with a place bearing the name « La Moinerie ». According to the very legendary *Vie de St Magloire* (Life of St Magloire), after having abandoned his position as bishop of Dol-de-Bretagne to become a hermit, Magloire is said to have received half of Sark's territory in gratitude for having healed one of the area's counts. Magloire consequently built a small chapel, cleared the surrounding land and planted wheat. To grind it, he built a water-mill and a small dam. The stream which flows alongside the Moinerie and is retained by "L'Ecluse" gushes down towards the beach which is still referred to as the "Port du Moulin". The foundation was to develop and St Magloire rapidly found himself in charge of 62 monks from Brittany, Neustria and Great Britain. A school was even built for the children of noble families from the Cotentin. St Magloire died in 586; however his monastery continued to prosper over several centuries.

The lovely present-day Moinerie, a farmhouse converted into a hotel, dates from 1728.

The Port du Moulin.

St Magloire's « post mortem » tribulations

Around the year 850, St Magloire's relics, which had been kept on the island, were victim to abduction by other monks!
Six Breton monks, on behalf of their king, Nominoe, who was seeking the protection of saintly relics, travelled to the island and rapidly won the confidence of Magloire's disciples.

Around midnight, the chief of the band of thieves, named Condon, seized the saint's coffin which, by a further miracle, was transported by invisible hands. The Breton monks could then take to the sea with their precious and pious plunder. Whilst the Sarkese were on the verge of catching up with the robbers, St Magloire, ungrateful towards his obstinate followers, had a violent storm strike the waters, forcing them to retreat to their island. Hence, the Royal Priory of St Magloire was created in Lehon.

The death of its protective saint and the disappearance of his relics were to mark the beginning of hard times on Sark. The frequent incursions and pillaging by bands of Nordic pirates who infested the waters at the time were to result in the disappearance of the monastery, making way for anarchy and barbarism.

The first mention of the island in a chart dates from 1042, when William, Duke of Normandy and future Conqueror, conceded Sark, together with Alderney to the Mont Saint-Michel abbey. Sark was then given by William to Geoffrey de Montbray, Bishop of Coutances and one of his loyal councillors. The latter was to lose Sark in 1093, together with his other fiefs, for having taken part in the Norman barons' rebellion following the Conqueror's death. Indeed, the barons had possessions on both sides of the Channel and were, consequently, in favour of the reunification of England and the Dukedom, which had been separated upon William the Conqueror's death, between his two eldest sons, Robert, Duke of Normandy and William Rufus, King of England. The barons took sides with Robert and were beaten by William Rufus. The question was to face the Norman lords once more two centuries later, as we know, with the permanent separation of England and the Dukedom, which had been reunited during the reign of Henry Beauclerc, William's third son.

The fief of Sark was therefore conceded by Henry Beauclerc to Richard de Redvers, one of his faithful companions, who in turn bequeathed the island to his son William de Vernon. In his later life, William donated the revenue from his land and the watermill on Sark to the Abbot of Montebourg, provided that the latter keep a monk on the island in charge of reciting mass to ensure that his soul, together with those of his kin, rest in peace. This solitary monk was referred to as the Prior of St Magloire; however did not live as St Magloire had, within a community, but as a hermit.

After the invasion of the dukedom by Philip Augustus, the Vernon family swore allegiance to the King of France and permanently lost its fief which was recovered by the British Crown.

Over the years that were to follow, Sark was the theatre of incessant raids. The island was occupied several times by Eustache the Monk, first of all on behalf of the King of England, then of the King of France. It was only after 1218 that the island regained a certain serenity, when governed by D'Aubigny, the Guardian of the Isles on behalf of the British Crown. Throughout the century, agriculture and conger fishing provided for the island's small community of 300 to 400 inhabitants. However, these good times were but short lived!

Eperquerie was fortified by François Bruel in 1549.

The Hundred Years' War brought new and continuous pillaging to the island, together with new periods of occupation by the French. Sark, completely devastated, was finally abandoned by its inhabitants and only wild rabbits continued to live there, soon to be joined by pirates and wreckers! The island's reputation was accurately described by Rabelais in the 16th Century, « *I saw the isles of Sark and Herm between Brittany and England... Isles of pirates, thieves, bandits, murderers and assassins... By the death of the wooden ox, I swear they are worse than cannibals. They would eat us alive!* ».

In 1549, King Henry II of France attacked the island with a fleet of 12 galleys and 13 further vessels which went on to ravage the north coast of Jersey. A band of some 200 French drunkards landed in Sark with their commander Captain François Bruel, occupied the island without being challenged and built three small forts at Eperquerie, Quenevets Castle on the point overlooking Dixcart Bay and at Vermondaye in Little Sark. However, four years later, the French, many of whom had deserted, were ousted out of the island by a Flemish corsair, Adrian Crole, assisted by 4 pilots from Guernsey. The island was soon deserted once more, after the attempted establishment there by Glatigny, a Cotentin lord, who finally abandoned following a new upsurge of hostilities between France and England.

Formidable reefs, like the Autelets pictured here, surround an island which is feared for its wreckers!

The Lords' era

In 1564, to remediate this somewhat volatile situation, whilst his own fief, St Ouen in Jersey was in a particularly vulnerable position should a French attack be made from Sark, Helier de Carteret, Seigneur of St Ouen, decided, upon a personal initiative and at his own expense, but having obtained the agreement of the Royal Commissioners and the Governor of Guernsey, to colonise the islands with a few families from his fief.

It was an ambitious venture since the abandoned island offered no source of income, its entire landscape covered with undergrowth requiring to be cleared. After having cultivated one field, as a test, Helier was delighted to produce an abundant harvest the following year. This result encouraged him in his endeavour to develop the island. Queen Elizabeth, sensitive to Helier de Carteret's work which reinforced the Crown's influence within the archipelago, conferred upon him by Letters Patent the title of Hereditary Seigneur of Sark, provided that at least 40 men remain on the island on a permanent basis to ensure its defence.

To satisfy the Queen's demand, Helier de Carteret divided the island into 40 properties comprising the seigneurial estate and 39 sub-fiefs or "tenements" which he conceded to his companions. Each tenement comprised a portion of

Each tenement comprised a portion of coastline to be defended.

coastline to defend, sufficient surrounding arable land to feed a family and pastures on the cliff tops. These tenements were provided in perpetual tenure; however, in return Helier's companions were to pay an annual tithe and to look after a house, and they had the added obligation of providing a man armed with a musket and ammunition to defend the island. Finally, the colonists were reunited within a consultative assembly, called the Chief Pleas, in charge of helping the Seigneur to govern the island. Helier established his own « tenure » in the centre of the island and entrusted 4 tenements, with additional hunting rights, to Nicholas Gosselin, the Guernsey Bailiff's son, as a token of his gratitude. The latter had considerably contributed to the success of his venture.

The Seigneur of St Ouen had all the new colony's necessary supplies transported from Jersey: horses, livestock, ploughing machines and seeds.

The island's first constructions sprung up and trees were planted. Little by little, a mill, homes on each tenure and roads were developed. Defensive work was carried out at Eperquerie whose name reminds us that the site was used to dry conger eels on stakes ("perches" in French) planted in the ground. It was also a landing spot, before the first tunnel was hollowed out to reach a new harbour in an east coast bay, only completed in 1588.

The island's new community, essentially composed of Jerseyan families, but also of Guernseyans and English families, was rapidly and closely united by the common practice of the new Presbyterian faith. In 1572, Helier travelled to London, where he met with the Queen, who conferred the status of Fief Haubert upon the island of Sark, in other words, under the authority of the sovereign, but independent from St Ouen, offering him 6 cannons to ensure its defence. Furthermore, the Seigneur was required to pay an annual rent of 50 sols tournois to the Queen's tax collector in Guernsey.

The first manor, a simple farm, was Helier de Carteret's residence.

One of the cannons given to Helier de Carteret by Queen Elizabeth I in 1572.

The Manor built during the 17th century.

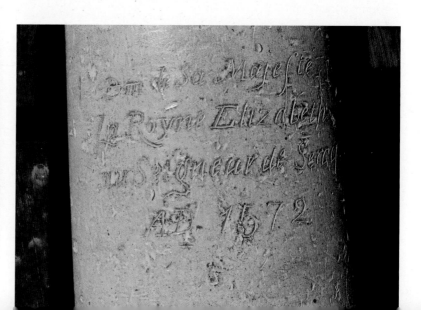

The Seigneurie, the Seigneurs' new official residence as from 1730.

After having established durable colonisation and development on Sark, Helier de Carteret bequeathed the island to his son, Philip in 1579. Helier retired to his estates in St Ouen; however he maintained a keen interest in Sark's development, attempting, though in vain, to have it transformed into a new bailiwick, independent from Guernsey.

When the Civil War broke out in England, the Seigneur of Sark was forced to leave the island which was in turn governed by a representative from the States of Guernsey, Captain Nicholas Ling. At the beginning of the Restoration, the Carteret's were able to return to their Seigneurie, which they succeeded in holding onto till 1713, when the island was given to a distant cousin from England. The latter resold the island in 1720 to Colonel Johnson, who had for many years been at the head of the Guernsey garrison. Sark was then to be passed on for a few years to another Englishman, James Milner. After his death, the island was resold, in 1730, to Suzanne Le Pelley, whose deceased husband was from a long-established Guernsey family.

The new Dame, who already owned La Perronerie, decided to take up residence there rather than moving to the Manor. Henceforth, La Perronerie became the Seigneurie and a dovecote was erected within the vicinity of the property symbolising the exclusive privilege endowed upon the owner of the Fief Haubert. Nevertheless, the Le Pelley family only used Sark as its summer residence, preferring to live the rest of the year in Guernsey.

The La Perronerie dovecote, built after the Seigneurie was transferred there in 1730.

Barracks built on Little Sark.

Despite internal discord, Sark remained ready for action.

The French Revolutionary ideas which were spreading across the islands were to result in internal discord on Sark with regard to the Seigneurial powers, whilst, on the religious front, clashes emerged between Methodists and Anglicans. This dissension had arisen at a time when the islands were particularly threatened, hence the necessity to reinforce the defensive measures in place on Sark and elsewhere. Furthermore, during the Napoleonic Wars, barracks were built on Little Sark to house a small detachment of English troops from a garrison posted in Guernsey. A station was also built to ensure the visual telegraph link between Alderney and Guernsey. And finally, the militia was re-equipped.

Following the discovery, in 1833, of copper and even silver loads on Little Sark, a mining company was set up to extract them. Some 250 miners arrived on the island from Cornwall. Four wells were dug to a depth of 200 yards, in other words 130 yards below sea level, with massive lateral galleries running alongside the silver vein. Several pumps and expensive machines were purchased. The young Seigneur Pierre Le Pelley, a descendant of the first Dame of Sark, provided funding for the company which announced the discovery of increasingly rich mineral deposits, requesting further capital.

Former mine chimney.

Following his brother's death in a shipwreck, Ernest became Seigneur, inheriting his wealth and investing further in the mining company which continued its activities, but which met with a number of successive incidents. A highly valuable stock of silver was lost at sea, the deepest galleries, where the richest minerals were to be found, became flooded and had to be abandoned. The Seigneur of Sark, to compensate for the banks who now refused any further investment and to allow the mining to continue, had no choice but to mortgage the island, with consent from the Crown. He did so against a

Plaque in memory of Pierre Le Pelley, who drowned on the 1st of March 1839, Sark church.

The Seigneurs of Sark

1565 .... Helier de Carteret
1581 .... Philip de Carteret (son)
1594 .... Sir Philip de Carteret (son)
1643 .... Sir Philip de Carteret, Bart (son)
1663 .... Sir Philip de Carteret, Bart (son)
1693 .... Sir Charles de Carteret, Bart (son)
1715 .... Lord John Carteret, (cousin), sold the fief.
1720 .... Colonel John Johnson
1723 .... James Milner bought the fief after the death of J. Johnson.
1730 .... Bishop of Gloucester, J. Milner's executor, sold the fief.
1730 .... Susanne Le Pelley
1733 .... Nicolas Le Pelley (son)
1742 .... Daniel Le Pelley (brother)
1752 .... Pierre Le Pelley (son)
1778 .... Pierre Le Pelley (son)
1820 .... Pierre Le Pelley (son)
1839 .... Ernest Le Pelley (brother)
1849 .... Peter Carey Le Pelley (son), sold the fief.
1852 .... Dame Marie Collings (née Allaire)
1853 .... Reverend William Thomas Collings (son)
1882 .... William Frederick Collings (son)
1937 .... Dame Sibyl Hathaway (daughter, née Collings)
1974 .... John Michael Beaumont (grandson)

The new tunnel initiated by Reverend William Collings.

The Seigneurie tower, built by Reverend William Collings.

loan of £4,000, to Jean Allaire, who was believed to be the richest man on Guernsey, having earned his fortune during the Napoleonic Wars thanks to privateering and, according to hearsay, piracy.

The mines were abandoned in 1847 and Ernest died, poverty stricken, two years later. In 1852, Marie, Jean Allaire's daughter and Thomas Geurin Collings' widow, foreclosed the mortgage inherited from her father and, after having obtained permission from the Crown, bought the fief from Pierre Carey Lepelley for the sum of £6,000, the value of the mortgage and interest payments having been deduced. Hence she became the second Dame of Sark; however only for 5 months! Her son, Reverend William Thomas Collings succeeded her for 29 years, considerably embellishing the Seigneurie and building the rather curious tower which still stands. He nevertheless continued, as had the Le Pelleys, to only use the island during the summer months, spending the winter with his family on Guernsey. However, he continued to take an interest in the island's development. He became aware of the great tourist potential for the island's economy and, despite reluctance from the Tenants, had a new harbour built to replace the breakwater at Creux Harbour, which had been destroyed by a series of violent storms during the winter of 1865, and had a new tunnel hollowed to facilitate its access. His son William succeeded him, becoming the first Seigneur to take up permanent residence on the island for 45 years up to his death in 1927.

As early as 1850, Sark welcomed its first tourists, who had come to visit the mines. The phenomenon was to develop thanks to the island's splendid landscapes and its wild cliffs, perfectly in keeping with the Romantic Canons on the beauty of nature, very much in vogue during the Victorian period. During his long exile on Guernsey, the French poet Victor Hugo paid frequent visits to Sark which was also a source of inspiration for many artists.

Sark's wild cliffs have attracted visitors
since the mid 19th Century.

The development of tourism, together with the presence of many miners from Cornwall, was to encourage the use of the English language, to the detriment of the locally spoken "Norman French" dialect. During the second half of the 19th Century, English was increasingly spoken, although the island's permanent population persevered with the local dialect. In 1889, an offer to purchase the fief to build a casino was thankfully declined by William Collings.

But Sark was also to experience another mutation, of a sociological nature: in 1890, only one tenement was held by a non-islander, whereas in 1914, ten tenements were held by families from outside Sark. The influx of immigrants who became permanent residents therefore transformed the island community, leading to, in 1922, the reform of the composition of the Chief Pleas assembly, by adding 12 Deputies voted in by the entire population.

Display depicting the occupation (German Occupation Museum, Sark).

Steamship in Creux Harbour.

Gun set up in the Sark countryside, abandoned by the Germans and preserved in the Seigneurie park.

Agriculture was on the decline, particularly wheat growing, under severe competition from low cost wheat imported from Canada and the United States, where production was on the increase. In Sark, this decline was not compensated for via the development of greenhouse cultivation, as was the case in Guernsey. It was consequently to result in the exodus of Sark's young population, looking for employment in the neighbouring isles or further afield. The island's male population decreased by 40 between 1891 and 1901, whence it comprised only 244 men. The island's total population was around 500.

William Collings' daughter, Dame Sybil Hathaway, succeeded her father in 1927. Married to an American who had been granted British citizenship, she developed Sark's tourist activity which was to become the island's main source of income. In 1938, she undertook to build a harbour in Maseline, accessible in all tidal conditions; however construction was interrupted by the onset of World War II.

The arrival of the German troops on the 3rd of July 1940 was to mark the start of foreign occupation, a situation that the island had not experienced since the 16th Century! The former Manor became the German command's headquarters. Mercifully, the occupants did not judge it necessary to fortify the island, thanks to its natural defences. Sybil Hathaway spoke German and was soon to become the only person on the island capable of courageously facing the occupant. Indeed, consequently to the 1942 raid on the Casquets by a British commando, the Dame's husband, together with the island's other British-born residents, had been deported to Germany where they were imprisoned.

Day-to-day life on Sark, although less restless than on the other islands, was nevertheless far from simple under the yoke of the occupant who established a curfew and limited fishing to specific

Dame Sybil Hathaway at the Seigneurie, facing German officers (German Occupation Museum, Sark).

times of the day. Gradually, every-day commodities were all lacking and the absence of the products imported during peacetime affected both the islanders and the occupant.

Thankfully, the German troops based in Sark signed their surrender on the 10th of May 1945.

The Germans surrendering (German Occupation Museum, Sark).

Plaque commemorating the 50th anniversary of the Liberation, on the front of the former school, today the Chief Pleas assembly.

The Fief Haubert institutions

In 1947, the island welcomed 20,000 visitors and the new Maseline harbour was completed, then officially inaugurated in 1949 by the Duke of Edinburgh. As in the other Channel Islands, the island's administration was reformed after harbours, a regular subject of discord, was replaced by the payment of a tax; the Seigneur's right of veto was cancelled should the Chief Pleas reapprove the contested measure within a period of 21 days. Nevertheless, the separation income, which now relied essentially on resources from outside the island, was gradually separated from public funds with the disappearance of tithes, milling taxes, contributions in the form of live poultry (known as the *poulade*) and

Cart used for the last tithe collected in Sark (Seigneurie park).

Entrance to the Court of the Chief Pleas and the Seneschal.

a number of other taxes paid to the Seigneur. Although the Seigneur's powers were considerably reduced, he nevertheless preserved certain privileges dating from the feudal period including the *droit de colombier* (possession of a dovecote). On the contrary, the exclusive authorisation to own a dog able to procreate does not stem from any feudal privilege but dates from the 17th Century, when an excessive number of errant dogs proved to be problematic for sheep breeding, following successive attacks on herds. In principle, the Seigneur also received the Treizième, a duty equivalent to one thirteenth of the value of any property sold on the island; howe-

World War II. For Sark, the public accounts were to be published annually; the corve due by Tenants for the maintenance of roads and of judicial from legislative power has not been adopted in Sark, as it has on the other islands.

Over the years, the seigneurial

ver, in 2007, he relinquished his right to personally receive this tax, in favour of the Chief Pleas.

Land ownership is governed by Letters Patent dating from 1611 and is based on inheritance by male primogeniture: Only the eldest son (up to 1999) may inherit land, in order to prevent parcels from being separated, hence potentially jeopardising the obligation to correctly defend and develop the island. Should a proprietor die without heirs, his land becomes the property of the Seigneur. If a tenement is sold to a person outside the hereditary family, any relative may exert his/her right of *retrait lignager*, in other words the right to regain possession of the property by reimbursing the purchaser.

This measure has proved to be a particularly efficient obstacle against rapacious property developers. Finally, up to a recent law, the islanders were not allowed to divorce, in order to avoid any interference with regard to inheritance. Today, there is still no specific divorce law in force on Sark; however, divorces proclaimed outside the island are acknowledged.

The Chief Pleas votes on taxation, checks the state of the island's finances, controls the day to day administration by means of committees, and holds legislative power. It is chaired by the Seneschal, who is appointed by the Seigneur for a period of 3 years. The Seneschal, together with the Seigneur, the 39 Tenants, the 12 Deputies of the People and the 5 officers collectively comprise the

Chief Pleas, the former exercising the casting vote when "pour" (for) and "contre" (against) votes are evenly balanced. A very recent institutional reform, which will be discussed later, has modified the assembly's composition.

The Seneschal is also in charge of justice, having taken an oath before the Court of Guernsey. He deals with civil and criminal affairs, the latter being more frequently referred to the Court of Guernsey.
The Seneschal's Court is the island's only court of justice and procedures there arc still based on Norman customary law.
The Seneschal acts as Judge for civil affairs and as Magistrate for criminal affairs. He is assisted by a Greffier acting as Clerk of the Court and by a Prévôt who executes the court's judgements.

The island's new school and Island Hall, inaugurated on the 21st of July 2005 by the Duke of York.

Once the Seigneur has appointed a Seneschal, he loses all power over him, becoming publically accountable and subject to trial like any other islander. The Seigneur can even be brought before his own court; this is precisely what happened to William Collings on several occasions from 1892 to 1903, owing to his conflicting relationships or his irreverent language with several islanders.

The 5 officers, who do not have the right to vote unless they are Tenants, include the Prévôt, the Greffier, the Treasurer, the Constable and the Vingtenier. The Prévôt collects the fines imposed by the Seneschal and watches over the incarceration of prisoners in the island's small prison. The Greffier is in charge of the island's public records and electoral roll; he registers deeds of public interest and orders voted by the Chief Pleas.
The Treasurer is in charge of the

Cars are not allowed on Sark.

island's finances. The Constable and the Vingtenier, among other functions, are in charge of ensuring public security and arrest the perpetrators of offenses.

Sark's public funds are modestly sufficient to satisfy the island's needs, relying on relatively low taxes levied on land and capital, alcohol and tobacco, and on landing

duties charged to the many tourists who visit Sark each year.

Sark has thus for a long time succeeded in remaining partly secluded from the outside world, refusing by the same token to welcome cars, forbidding anyone from flying over its territory and rejecting a proposed helicopter service from Guernsey.

Tractors are used for agriculture, but horses are more than welcome on Sark, particularly for horse-drawn carriage rides which are very popular among tourists.

Towards the demise of Europe's last feudal state

This particular way of life and these institutions, marked by the passage of time and perfectly accepted by the island's community, have over the last few years been challenged by two tremendously rich businessmen, the Barclay brothers, owners since 1993 of a particular tenure, the island of Brecqhou, on which they have had an immense and luxurious pseudo-medieval castle built, including a helicopter launch pad!

These two billionaires, Sir David and Fredrick Barclay, knighted in the year 2000 for their support for medical research, own The Telegraph Group which includes the Daily Telegraph, together with the Ritz Hotel in London.They believe that Sark's legislation requires to be modernised, going as far as to challenge its legality, since it allows them neither to dispose of Brecqhou as they wish, nor to pass the island on to their 4 children. For the same reason, their lawyers have declared war against Sark's institutions, starting with the principle of primogeniture, the grounds of which they have challenged before the European Court of Human Rights.

Sark, although not a member of the European Community, nevertheless ratified the European Convention on Human rights in 1982. The European Court ruled in favour of the British tycoons in 1999 and the Chief Pleas had no choice but to alter Sark's law of succession.
However, the Barclays' battle is not yet over! They intend to conti-

Brecqhou, which is still referred to as L'Ile aux Marchands.

nue their efforts to democratise Sark's institutions.

Fearing the total loss of the island's specificity, the Chief Pleas finally considered revising its constitution, whilst remaining deeply attached to its Tenants who perpetuate tradition, contrary to newcomers to the island. The latter, essentially wealthy English people coming to retire to the island for a few years, are unfamiliar with local habits, have difficulty in integrating into the island community, many of them rapidly returning home, unable to adapt to this rather peculiar universe.

On the 6th of September 2006, Sark's inhabitants were officially consulted with regard to the composition of the Chief Pleas: 56% voted in favour of the principle of 28 open seats. Consequently, on the 4th of October 2006, the Chief Pleas voted the principal of a totally elected parliament by universal suffrage.This resolution will be subject to a referendum within 4 years.During the transitory period, the Chief Pleas' 28 seats will be shared among 16 Tenants and 12 Deputies.The present-day Seigneur, Michael Beaumont, grandson and successor to the former Dame of Sark since 1974, has conserved very limited powers, far from the feudalism adopted on the island for centuries and ensuring its longevity to this very day as a lively and extremely original community. However, Sark has benefited from the Barclays' entrepreunerial experience and their financial involvement has contributed towards the island's tourist potential, through the renovation of shops and hotels.

Walks in the heart of the island

Sark can be visited by foot, bike or horse-drawn carriage. Lovely untarred roads, with the exception of the abrupt 800m Amont du Creux road (also known as Harbour Hill) linking the harbours to the island's interior, meander pleasantly across Sark's verdant and luxuriant landscape.

The La Collinette crossroads, where horse-drawn carriages await the island's visitors, also leads to Sark's high street, somewhat pompously referred to as The Avenue. In fact, it is a pleasant country road, bordered by a few houses and modest stores, but it is also one of the reasons Sark is so charming, so distant from a dense urban environment! Once past the Post Office, visitors can continue westwards towards the Pilcher Monument or the Havre Gosselin, named after Helier de Carteret's companion, or bear northwards, to discover the parish church built in 1820 then, after the fire station which also houses the ambulance towed by a tractor, the former school with its bell, where the Chief Pleas meet three times yearly, mid January, at Easter and at Michaelmas.

A curious window.

La Collinette with its horse-drawn carriages awaiting visitors.

Sark's traditional houses.

The Avenue with its shops and its typically country atmosphere, in keeping with the island's personality.

The Post Office.

The parish church of St Peter.

St Peter's parish church was built following the creation of a specific fund for the construction of Anglican churches by the British government, alarmed by the rapid propagation of Methodism, regarded in many circles as a subversive movement. The Seigneur of Sark had the idea of restoring the Anglican church's prestige, taking advantage of the grants awarded, to which he added the profits of a sale of church benches to the island's Tenants.

Each church bench has its own embroidered cushion, including the one intended for potential prisoners who are entitled to attend church services, in the company of the Constable.

Tapestry relating Sark's major historical events, embroidered by the "Thursday Club" in 1977-1978 and displayed in the church.

In the cemetery, many names can be found of Helier de Carteret's first companions, such as Hamon for example. In 1565, Thomas Hamon was the first tenant of La Valette de Haut.

Those having followed the west road, rather than branching off towards the church, will rapidly discover a series of interesting buildings.

First of all, they will find the tiny prison, built in 1856, not far from the former arsenal and beside an old school, today converted into an information centre and the headquarters of the Sark Society. The prison only has two cells; what's more, the Seneschal may only pronounce a sentence of a maximum of two day's imprisonment. Longer penalties must be brought before the Royal Court of Guernsey.

A little further on, to the right, the Manor, the former Seigneurial residence, is a beautiful granite house built in the 18th Century, in a style in keeping with Jersey farms. The early manor, built by Helier de Carteret, is situated on the right side opposite the old school, forming a band of small bungalows, similar to the early Jersey Farms.

The Carteret coat of arms on the 17th Century Manor.

Sark prison, built on the initiative of W.T. Collings, Seigneur of Sark.

If they continue westward, after having walked past the mill, the road then the path lead to the Pilcher Monument and to the Havre Gosselin anchorages, the only landing zone on the west coast, accessible by means of a long flight of steps. A granite obelisk has been erected on the cliff top in memory of the wreck of a small boat travelling back to Guernsey during the winter of 1886 with, on board, a rich London merchant, Jeremiah Pilcher. The site offers splendid views out to the Havre Gosselin, Brecqhou, then Herm, Jethou and Guernsey.

The Seigneurial mill.

Dixcart Hotel, visited by Victor Hugo.

The Dixcart Bay arch.

Havre Gosselin and the Island of Brecqhou.

Approximately 200m from there stands the old mill, today deprived of its vanes, also built by Helier de Carteret and restored after the Liberation, since the Germans had transformed it into an observation tower. Traces of the Carteret coat of arms are still visible on the stone lintel above the door. Consequent to ideas propagated during the French Revolution, certain feudal rights had been challenged in Sark, among which the Seigneur's milling monopoly. Initially questioned by Thomas Carteret, Tenant of La Forge, who built a mill in 1796, this right was soon to be contested once more by the Tenant of La Piperie. The latter built another mill on Little Sark, of which only ruins remain today, for himself and his neighbours, pretexting that it was often too difficult and hazardous to cross La Coupee in reason of its poor maintenance.

To the left of the Manor, a lane leads to Dixcart Valley and via a path, which meanders through a picturesque wood, walkers reach Dixcart Bay with its curious rocky arch detached from the cliff. Immediately prior to reaching the bay, they will have noticed the Dixcart Hotel, where Victor Hugo used to stay during his frequent visits to Sark.

The Seigneurie and, to the right, the seigneurial chapel.

Ducks in the pond, originally a reservoir developed by the monks for the watermill located downstream.

Stone pigeon in the Seigneurie park.

Inscription on the entrance gates to the Seigneurie.

In 1730, the Seigneurie was moved by Susanne Le Pelley to the tenure called La Perronerie of which she was already the owner, and which was also the site of the former St Magloire priory. The main building very probably dates back to 1675, as testified by the date engraved in the dining room's granite fireplace. The house was extended by Susanne Le Pelley's son, to be further embellished by Reverend W.T. Collings, Seigneur from 1853 to 1882, who added a large lounge and a square tower. The banner that flies above the tower is that of the Seigneur. It depicts two golden Normandy leopards on a red background, in the canton of a cross of St George, the same cross that can be found on the flags of Guernsey and Alderney.

Due to successive constructions and extensions, it is difficult to find one's bearing in this beautiful residence which, to complicate matters even further, comprises no less than sixteen interior staircases, excluding the one in the tower! Since the Seigneurie is the Seigneur's permanent place of residence, it is not open to the public, contrary to its magnificent park and gardens.

The walled garden, protected from storms and frost, is even considered to be one of the Channel Islands' finest.

One of the Channel Islands' most beautiful gardens, thanks to Dame Sibyl Hathaway.

The Window in the Rock.

From the Seigneurie, a path through a small wood leads to the Port du Moulin bay (whose name is reminiscent of St Magloire's watermill), one of the island's most spectacular, and to a peculiar opening hollowed out in the reef and known as The Window in the Rock.

At the island's most northerly headland, the Eperquerie peninsula, a vast moorland with remarkable flowers, ferns and heathers, reaches its extremity at the Bec du Nez reefs. Several small pathways lead the way down to the coast and to the natural haven of Eperquerie, where Helier de Carteret and his colonists landed. Other paths make their way to the tip of the promontory, where the ruined section of a wall, formerly part of a tower, can be seen next to the local militia's former firing ground. Nearby, a narrow gully marks the entrance to the impressive Boutique Caves, accessible at low tide. Other caves can also be visited around Fontaines Bay, on the east coast of Eperquerie.

The Eperquerie peninsula.

The Grève de la Ville pathway.

Among the other possible walks - and they are countless – a short stroll to La Grève de la Ville, on the east coast, offers access to an exceptional site. A gently descending path, via a series of curves between the embankments, ends in a flight of steps leading to the beach, from where the Chapelle aux Mauves (Seagulls in Norman dialect) can be seen.
It is an astonishing example of natural architecture with its sloping roof and cave.

The Grève de la Ville and the Chapelle aux Mauves.

La Coupee was, for a long time, but a narrow pathway devoid of any parapet to ensure a safe crossing.

Duval Farm on Little Sark.

The La Coupee causeway today.

the foot of La Coupee, dreadful lamentations and groaning can sometimes be heard, akin to souls lost in hell. For those seeking reassurance, such howlings are said to be the product of a simple medley of tide and wind!

In his « notebook » on the 8th of June 1859, Victor Hugo recalled, in a few terse yet highly evocative lines, this extraordinary site under harsh weather conditions, « *La Coupee. Storm out to sea, cormorants, gulls, cries, sinister flight – white on the sea, black in the sky – Guernsey hazy, Jersey faint – deep fog – outline of the abyss plunging violently into darkness to my right – obscure thunderbolt in the night - a sudden, vast and desperate flash of lightning – above my head the wild oats shudder on the edge of the ravine* ».

However, Sark's most extraordinary site is undoubtedly La Coupee, a ridge providing access to Little Sark. This high and narrow rocky crest, barely 3 metres wide in certain places, is bordered on both sides by vertiginous precipices. The crossing remains somewhat terrifying, despite a solid concrete causeway, replacing the former rudimentary pathway, which was even narrower.

The present-day causeway was built by German prisoners of war in 1945, under the command of the British Royal Engineers. At an altitude of 60 metres above sea level, the ridge is nevertheless lower than the two parts of the island it reunites. In 1811, then again in 1862, landslides rendered the pathway too narrow for it to be safely negotiable, and it was consequently lowered to offer a wider base. Finally, in 1900, since there was no parapet, children who had to cross La Coupee on their way to school had to do so on their knees on windy days. Since then, from the caves at

Vestiges of the former mines.

La Grande Grève, seen from La Coupee, and Brecqhou. On the horizon, Guernsey, Jethou and Herm.

Sheep in Rouge Terrier on Little Sark, with the islet of Moie de Breniere out to sea.

Les Fontaines Bay.

Once La Coupee has been crossed, Little Sark invites a lingering stroll throughout its roads and pathways. After Duval Farm and the picturesque hamlet of Little Sark, a lane leads to the Venus Pool, a natural rock cavity which holds back the sea water even at low tide. Another path opening out into a field leads to the Rouge Terrier dolmen, and another to the ruins of the former silver mines and Port Gorey, from where the minerals were shipped.

A multitude of other footpaths are just waiting to be discovered on Great Sark, such as the superb Hog's Back offering splendid views of both Derrible Bay and Dixcart Bay, or the equally charming path running alongside Les Fontaines Bay, or another passing nearby the Pointe Robert Lighthouse, within the natural and totally preserved paradise forming this peaceful island, where each landscape unfolds, more beautiful than the last.

An enclosed field gate.

Pointe Robert Lighthouse and the Grande Moie rocks.

Car ferry in the St Helier harbour channel;
to the right Hermitage Rock with the ruins of a fort and the
chapel erected in the 12th Century in memory of St Helier.

Jersey,
the southerly British isle

When arriving in Jersey onboard one of the high-speed catamarans which now provide links between the Norman and Breton harbours and St Helier, the island's capital, one can but be slightly disappointed by the harbour side with its lines of modern buildings of controversial architectural inspiration, alongside the Fort Regent leisure centre's immense white dome which overlooks the town. To the right, the power station's high chimney stands out on the skyline, despite the fact that the island's electricity supply is provided by the EDF (French electricity board) station in Flamanville, on the Cotentin peninsula.

St Helier and its surroundings.

However, if you are lucky to sail into Jersey on a yacht via Gorey harbour, on the east coast, or St Aubin, to the west of St Helier, you are sure to marvel at the sheer beauty of these two coastal sites. So, Jersey is an island of many faces. After the initial disappointment of the sea approach to St Helier, visitors discover a large town buzzing with activity, living at a hectic pace, with incessant traffic and crowded pedestrian streets. Thankfully, the town centre has preserved its original charm and, of course, across the island, its scenic landscapes and, in particular, the magnificent north coast, still wild and safeguarded from the urban development which is gradually spreading across the island's south coast, eating into the over-looking hills.

With its 91,000 inhabitants, Jersey is, indeed, both the largest of the islands in the archipelago and the most extensively developed, relying on banking, offshore finance and tourism. These activities ensure the island's prosperity, providing three quarters of its income. To satisfy the island's fresh water needs, Jersey has built a seawater desalination plant. Energy, food supplies and consumer goods are, for the best part, imported; however this does not prevent the island from enjoying its own flourishing economy.

Jersey is geographically the most southerly of the Channel Islands with a general shape reminiscent of a chunky rectangle with a large and deep bay in its centre, opening southwards; St Aubin's Bay. Fifteen kilometres long by eight kilometres wide, Jersey comprises a large and verdant plateau bordered, to the north, by high cliffs towering at 130m above sea level, interspersed with small picturesque harbours and gently sloping southwards towards the shore. The

The north coast with its outstanding cliffs.

island's other coasts are less precipitous, opening out onto long sandy bays.

Jersey is separated from the Cotentin peninsula by the 13 nautical mile La Déroute channel, whose sand banks reach zero level on nautical charts and stretch out towards the dangerous rocky plateau forming Les Ecrehou. To the south, towards Brittany and Saint-Malo, stands the vast plateau of the Minquiers, midway, with its hundreds of rocks emerging from the waters.

Today, at low tide, a depth of barely 10 metres separates Jersey from the Cotentin. However, the famous spring tide which is said to have separated the island from the Continent, together with the traditional belief that the Bishop of Coutances could reach Jersey by crossing a ford aboard a simple plank, are but simple legends!

St Aubin's Harbour.

Traces of life dating from Neanderthal man

Among all of the islands of the archipelago, Jersey is the most recently detached from the Continent, around 6000 years BC, and around 1,000 years after Guernsey, Sark and Alderney.

Conversely, the earliest traces of human life, dating from around 250,000 years ago, were found on Jersey. In the cave in La Cotte de Saint Brelade, archaeologists have unearthed the vestiges of the oldest prehistoric populations in Europe. At the time, the English Channel did not exist and Jersey was not yet an island!

The bones of animals found on the island confirm the presence of mammoths and hairy rhinoceros in the region. Several specimens had their skulls crushed, leading researchers to believe that Palaeolithic man pushed the animals off the cliff top. These hunter-collectors, contemporary to Neanderthal man, produced their weapons and tools from quartz and flint, to which hundreds of thousands of fragments found on the island bear witness.

During the Neolithic Period, Jersey was covered with menhirs and dolmens and the population, which very probably comprised Iberian then Celtic tribes, gradually settled. Several funerary sites remain from this period dating back some 6,000 years.

Among these megaliths, the most impressive is undeniably the Hougue Bie, whose name has been deformed from the original: Hougue Hambye. The Paisnels, an

La Hougue bie, surmounted by 2 chapels, side by side, the older of which may date from the 12th Century.

influential Norman family, lords of Hambye and proprietors of several fiefs in Jersey before Philip Augustus occupied Continental Normandy, had built a chapel on this large, 12 to 13 metre hillock (or hougue).

The main chamber at La Hougue Bie.

The La Hougue Bie dragon

The legend of the valorous lord of Hambye remains associated with this site, as recounted on bygone evenings, in Jèrriais, « *Un tèrrib'liye dragon vivait l'temp passé dans l'Mathais d'Saint Louothains et quand i'sortait faisait des ravages dans la campagne, en tuant à drouaite et à gauche. Les pouorres médgians tchi vivaient en Jèrri dans chu temps-là 'taient êpouvantés et craintifs jour et niet. Né v'là qué l'Seigneu d'Hambye, en Nourormandie, en eut l'vent siez li dans san châté d'Hambye et même nou l'suppliyit dé v'nin en Jèrri pour dêtruithe chutte laie et âffreuse bête* ».

Paisnel, a courageous knight from the Cotentin came to Jersey with his squire, to kill this fearsome monster. But, after succeeding in chopping off the head of this hideous beast, the wounded lord of Hambye, whilst taking a moment's respite, had his throat cut by his perfidious squire, seeking credit for his deed.

On his return to Hambye Castle, the squire explained that he had succeeded in killing the monster after the latter had seriously wounded his master, who, upon his last breath, had requested that his avenger marry his wife and succeed him as lord. By love for her husband, the lady accepted. However, the vile squire, haunted by guilt, was to reveal his act of treachery to his new wife, whilst speaking out loud in his sleep, « *Oh, what a villain I am, I have massacred my master!* ».

The treacherous criminal was hanged and the lady had a huge mound erected in Jersey, on the very spot of the crime, then had a chapel built for masses to be recited, so that the genuine lord's soul may rest in peace.

It was only in 1925 that the Société Jersiaise, the new owner of the Hougue Bie site, discovered that this large knoll was in fact artificial, protecting a major construction of huge blocks of granite comprising an immense funeral mound. Its existence would appear to prove that there was, among these Neolithic people, a form of social organisation exerting authority over a vast area stretching out to the coast. Indeed, the site was built using granite blocks eroded by the sea, hence proving that they were dragged from the east shores across a distance of 3 to 5km, very probably transported and installed by abundant manpower, by means of earthen ramps and wooden rollers.

This twenty metre long complex includes a 9 metre long access gallery leading to an oval chamber, 2 metres wide by 1.5 metres high, flanked by two small lateral chambers, to the left and right. The bones of 3 women and 5 men, together with fragments of pottery, have been found in the lateral chambers. Finally, above the main chamber, there is a smaller one, perhaps the sanctuary's most sacred place.

This prime Neolithic site, although generally regarded as a tomb, in fact served several purposes, only one of which was as a funeral chamber. It was used over several centuries before being permanently walled and abandoned. It has been noted, hence adding a further touch of mystery to the site, that during the spring and autumn equinoxes, the rising

The Dolmen du Mont Ubé.

sun illuminates this superb burial mound's gallery and main chamber.

La Pouquelaye de Faldouet.

The presence of over 30 dolmens has been recorded across Jersey, 14 of which remain today. Among them, the Dolmen du Mont Ubé, in the parish of St Clement, is located on the edge of a small wood. This dolmen was discovered in 1848, too late for the huge capstones to be saved; they had been hastily removed by quarrymen. All that remains are the vertical stones comprising the 5 metre long access corridor and the funeral chamber.

Another example, the Dolmen de La Pouquelaye de Faldouet, is situated in St Martin. Although mention was made of the site as early as 1682, it suffered less damage than its counterpart in Mont Ubé. Restored in the late 19th Century, this 14 metre long dolmen comprised a 5 metre formerly covered gallery, opening out onto two successive circular funeral chambers; an uncommon formation. The deeper of the two chambers, in the form of a horse-shoe, is still covered by an impressive 24 tonne capstone. It would appear that this chamber was in fact the original corridor. The first chamber is surrounded by small lateral chambers. The entire arrangement was originally surrounded by a low mound supported by two dry stone walls and a vertical stone circle. Fragments of pottery have been found on the site, together with two polished stone axes, two stone pendants and human bones.

It was near to this very dolmen that, in 1855, seven months before leaving Jersey, Victor Hugo wrote his poem *Nomen, Numen, Lumen,*

When he had done – when every scattered
Rose dazzled out of chaos in its place
And all of them were ordered in their far
Abodes – needing to name himself to
space,
The awesome serene Being rose up over
The darkness, towering, and cried out,
"JEHOVAH!"

At Le Pinacle, another of the island's sacred prehistoric sites, the remains of a fanum, a small Gallo-Roman temple, can be seen. However, very few other traces of the Roman period remain, apart from coins, bearing witness to the existence of trading.

In the 6th Century, evangelisers were increasingly numerous throughout the isles and, according to hagiographers, one of St Marcouf's disciples, a hermit named Helibert or Helier, settled on Jersey on a rock facing the south coast. This rock, located close to Elizabeth Castle, has since been named Hermitage Rock.

At the time the island had few inhabitants, following incessant pirate attacks. In 555, after 15 years of meditation, prayer and miracles, Helier was murdered, decapitated by pirates armed with axes, whilst attempting to protect the islanders. However, according to legend, Helier carried his own head towards the shore. This miraculous event terrorised the pirates who immediately took to the sea, hence saving the island from further ransacking!

A highly coveted island

The conquest of England in 1066 by Duke William was to link Jersey with England for the very first time, hence the witty claim by Jerseyans that England in fact belongs to Jersey and not the contrary! The great poet William Wace was born in Jersey in 1115,

Mont Orgueil Castle, engraving by J. Harwood, 1844.

The most important landings on the island from 1200 to 1549

(Source: Jersey Museum)

1205 .... Mercenaries led by Eustache the Monk ravaged the Channel Islands.

1215-1216 ...... Eustache occupied the Islands on behalf of the French.

1294 .... Around 1,500 islanders were killed during a French raid.

1336 .... David Bruce, the exiled King of Scotland led a French incursion.

1337 .... Beginning of the Hundred Years' War. The French, led by Sir Nicholas Behuchet, occupied the island for 6 months.

1338 .... A French army, said to comprise some 8,000 men, devastated the island.

1339 .... Three major incursions within the same year.

1372 .... The island was ravaged by a French troop led by the Prince of Wales.

1373 .... Bertrand du Guesclin, constable of France, invaded the island with a troop of 2,600 men.

1380-1382 ...... A French army, led by Jean de Vienne, occupied the island.

1403 .... A Breton fleet, under the orders of Admiral Jean De Pehouet, attacked the island.

1406 .... Pierre Hector de Pontbriand and Pero Nino carried out a major raid, together with 1,000 mercenaries.

1454 .... 500 islanders were declared dead following a French attack.

1461-1468 ...... French occupation under Jean de Carbonnel.

1549 .... A French invasion force was defeated at Jardin d'Olivet.

as his Roman de Rou, an epic devoted to the Norman Dukes, recounts,

"Jo di e dirai que jo sui
Wace de l'isle de Gersui
Qui est en mer vers occident
Al fieu de Normendie apent".

Following the separation of Continental Normandy from insular Normandy, although the Norman lords had fiefs in the isles, they had far more substantial possessions and income in France, hence their initial allegiance to Philip Augustus, just like the Guernseyans. John Lackland was subsequently forced into asking Eustache the Monk for help in reclaiming the islands.

Following the latter's success and certain Norman lords' loss of their insular wealth, the King of England was acknowledged in the islands as Duke of Normandy by the remaining Norman noblemen. If truth be told, however, to guarantee their loyalty, John Lackland had in fact taken several members of the island's most influential families hostage, including a leading figure from the Carteret family! Later, given time and the political skill of the successive British sovereigns, Jersey's loyalty to the British Crown was to become total, hence its cultural evolution and its history over the following centuries.

The Carterets, who were to play a particularly important role in the island's history, were originally from the small harbour town of Carteret, on the Cotentin peninsula, where they were the lords of the Manor and had taken part in the first crusade, then in the Battle of Hastings. Renaud de Carteret, who had sided with John Lackland and helped in defending Rouen in 1204, together with Pierre de Préaux, had no choice but to abandon his possessions in France in favour of his unique fief in Jersey, Saint Ouen. A little later, Gorey Castle, which was also to take on the name of Mont Orgueil in the 15th Century, was built to protect the island from French attack.

Its name is thought to originate from the great impression its location and its force made on Thomas, Duke of Lancaster and brother to King Henry V, who described it as such.

Jersey was attacked several times during the Hundred Years' War and was even occupied for a short period. At the Treaty of Brétigny, signed in 1360, the French agreed to relinquish the islands; however, raids resumed as early as 1372, as already mentioned in the chapter on Guernsey. The following year, Bertrand du Guesclin managed to overpower Gorey Castle's exterior defences, with help from Jean de Saint Martin, a Jerseyman in favour of the French intrusion, but he failed to enter the keep. The French, nevertheless, succeeded in occupying Grosnez Castle on the island's north-west headland. Over the years that were to follow, further raids were organised, forcing the islanders to pay ransoms in exchange for tranquillity. In 1380, the French Admiral Jean de Vienne took possession of Jersey, only to be forced out two years later.

In 1461, Jersey was to be occupied once more, for a period of seven years, by Norman captains led by Jean Carbonnel, Lord of

In the 14th Century, Mont Orgueil resisted several attacks (Statue of a knight in Mont Orgueil Castle's lower courtyard).

Sourdeval, acting on behalf of Pierre de Brezé, Count of Maulévrier and grand seneschal of Normandy. After his nocturnal arrival before Gorey Castle, Carbonnel entered the fortress with the complicity of the two Saint Martin brothers, who were friends of Jean Nenfant, the island's governor, who himself was startled from his very bed!

Grosnez Castle, to the north-west of the island.

Whilst he feigned resistance, the invaders jokingly teased, "You are but a child, go back to bed!" Although this pun did not go down in history, the Jerseyans remain to this very day indignant, as much at the governor's submissiveness as at this mediocre play on words.

It would appear, however, that Nenfant had in fact received orders from Margaret of Anjou, King Henry VI of England's queen consort, to allow the French to capture the castle.

Pierre de Brezé was proclaimed Seigneur of the isles, and promulgated orders confirming the island's franchises and bestowed legislative power to the States, whilst being supported by the Royal Court which dealt, not only with criminal affairs but which also drafted the island's laws. These texts also include the very first mention of "Mont Orgeuil", referring to Gorey Castle. But on the night of the 17th of May 1468, Admiral Richard Harliston's fleet arrived before Mont Orgueil with the aim of blockading the castle, with inland help from Philippe de Carteret's men. After a siege of over 5 months, Jean de Carbonnel was finally forced into surrender.

The island's immediate future was to prove harsh. The legislative power was returned to the Court, whilst Harliston, the new governor, maintained the best part of the island's power within his own hands, to the detriment of the Bailiff and the island's other representatives; at least until such times as he was forced to withdraw. Indeed, as a partisan of the House of York, Harliston refused to hand over the castle keys to King Henry VII's emissaries who, before the governor's opposition, besieged Mont Orgueil. Harliston was forced to flee, to the great satisfaction of the Jerseyans who gratefully recovered their freedom and their scorned privileges. However, conflict was soon to rearise between the island's new governors and its nobility.

Under the reign of Elizabeth I, as we have already read, Helier de Carteret, Seigneur of Saint Ouen, was granted the Seigneurie of Sark, provided that he colonise the uninhabited island in order to prevent the pirates, who were rife throughout the archipelago, from using it as their hideout.

Sir Walter Raleigh, a miniature by the painter Nicolas Hilliard.

The Queen's former favourite, Sir Walter Raleigh, was named governor of Jersey in 1600 and undertook to modernise the island's fortifications. Mont Orgueil was believed to be unsuitable for defence against recently developed cannons and a new fortress was built on an islet in St Aubin's Bay where St Helier's former abbey stood, to be named Elizabeth Castle in honour of the Queen.

Raleigh also incited the Jerseyans into developing fishing activities in Newfoundland, which was to bring relative affluence to the island during the first half of the 17th Century, and he introduced tobacco. However, the exportation of tobacco harvested in Jersey was prohibited as from 1624, since it competed directly with the Virginia plantations, owned by the British Crown. This prohibition was to result in fraudulent trade which persisted to the end of the 19th Century. The island's only industry, particularly meagre at the time, consisted in the manufacture of knitted stockings which enabled a large majority of its population to survive, occasionally to the detriment of agricultural activities, labourers failing to find sufficient manpower to assist them!

Whilst the Civil War was breaking out in England, Jersey's most influential Seigneur, the Bailiff Philippe de Carteret, publicly proclaimed his loyalty to the king, contrary to one of Jersey's other noble families, the Lemprières, who sided with Cromwell's Parliamentarians. During a particularly chaotic session of the States convened by the Bailiff, and within increasing commotion exacerbated by insults from friends of the Carterets, Michel Lemprière informed, on behalf of Parliament, of the request that Philippe de Carteret be arrested. Learning of the approach of the parish militia who were in support of the Parliamentarians, the Carteret finally fled the assembly to seek refuge in Elizabeth Castle together with his escort; however he died a few months later. His nephew, George Carteret (note that the nobiliary particle has been dropped), a renowned royal Navy officer, pursued the battle against the Parliamentarians and was granted by Charles I the simultaneous functions of Bailiff and Lieutenant-Governor in 1643.

Entrance to Elizabeth Castle.

George Carteret, a skilled seaman, was to arm several ships over the following eight years. Appointed Vice Admiral of Jersey and the maritime parts adjacent - hence avoiding him from being regarded as a simple pirate – he travelled up and down the English Channel with his squadron, capturing parliamentary ships and English merchant ships and bringing them back to Jersey, specifically to the haven of St Aubin, the island's main harbour at the time. St Helier did not have a genuine harbour and was as yet a muddy village; whilst communication within the island was extremely painstaking due to the very poor state of its roads and thoroughfares. It was nevertheless during the same period that the « Cohue » was built in St Helier; a building to house the Jurats' assembly, near to the market originally created by monks from the Abbey of St Helier and which attracted the island's peasants.

After the execution of his father, Prince Charles, who had become King of England and was exiled in France, embarked in Coutainville on his way to Jersey, where he had already stayed 3 months after his departure from England, with the intention of reconquering his kingdom. Charles was once more welcomed to Elizabeth Castle by George Carteret.

The latter had the prince, now King Charles II's presence on the island publicly announced on the market place and undertook to cover the Royal House's expenses, involving 300 people according to chronicles, readily levying extra taxes on the local population in complement to his own riches.

The fort which protects the haven of St Aubin.

In 1651, Sir George Carteret was forced to seek refuge in Elizabeth Castle.

George Carteret also provided support for the Royalist garrison confined to Castle Cornet in Guernsey by sending ships laden with supplies. However, in October 1651, Cromwell decided to put an end to this situation and sent Blake at the head of an 80 vessel fleet. Hence, the Parliamentary army landed on Jersey and forced Sir George to have himself locked up inside Elizabeth Castle. Mortar fire caused an explosion in the ammunition hold, killing many of the castle's defenders. The besieged surrendered in December, with the honours of war. George Carteret was authorised to arm a ship and to set sail for Saint-Malo.

Exiled in France, Carteret rejoined Charles II's court in Paris and, thanks to his resourcefulness, succeeded in obtaining a command post in the French Navy to continue his fight against the English fleet, until such times as Mazarin, increasingly close to Cromwell, had him imprisoned in the Bastille, before allowing him to leave to rejoin Charles II in Holland.

Sir George Carteret, Jersey postage stamp printed in 1976.

Meanwhile in Jersey, Michel Lemprière replaced George Carteret as Bailiff, despite the fact that the population remained more willingly royalist.

Upon his return to his kingdom in 1660, Charles II expressed his gratitude to George Carteret in the form of land within the new American colonies, which was to take on the name of New Jersey, a territory which has today become one of the United States. The island of Jersey received a royal mace in carved vermeil which has since been placed before the Bailiff's seat whenever he chairs a session of the States or of the Royal Court. The island was then to enjoy a prosperous period.

Jersey ready for action once more

In the 18th Century, Jersey was once more ready for action. As early as 1689, William III had repealed the principle of the islands' neutrality. Thus, the Jerseyans were not the last to transform their merchant ships into corsairs; George Carteret's bygone vocation could now be revived and flourish once more, this time in allegiance with British warships!

An increasing number of the island's 20,000 inhabitants were to turn to the sea for their livelihood. Whilst continuing their fishing activities in the Gulf of St Lawrence and Labrador, the

Martello tower at Le Hocq Point, built in 1781.

Archirondel Martello tower, built in 1793-94. Contrary to the Guernsey towers, Jersey's towers were larger and encircled with machicolations to ensure that the entire foot of the towers was accessible to defensive fire.

La Rocco Tower, built in 1798-98, Saint Ouen's Bay.

Martello tower, built in 1837, on the heights of St Catherine's Bay.
Its general plan was similar to those built on the east coast of England and was perfectly suitable for installing a carronade on the upper platform.
This tower located on the shores of Saint Ouen Bay was, together with Kempt Tower, among the last group of Martello towers to be built in Europe.

Jerseyans found new and extremely lucrative earnings, in both smuggling and in privateering. Trading of salt, tobacco and fabric, although illicit, proved to be far more profitable than traditional agricultural activities. The modest port of St Helier was to develop and to become richer thanks to the huge profits gained from smuggling and privateering. The local authorities were even led to limiting such activities, to ensure that the local militia was not divest of its manpower.

St Helier continued its demographic growth with an influx of French, but also English immigrants, who fled the taxies levied to compensate for the Napoleonic Wars, together with incoming British troops to man the garrison. The town's population grew from 2,000 in 1734 to 8,000 in 1800.

Jersey's seamen paid frequent visits to foreign ports and were particularly partial to the small archipelago of Chausey from where they could watch over the movements of the French ships. For a while, there was even a genuine Jerseyan industry in the Isles of Chausey during the first half of the 18th Century, with the arrival of over 300 labourers to extract the granite required for Jersey's building projects.

The island's defence was considerably reinforced in the last decades of the 18th Century, with the erection of 23 of the 30 planned Martello towers as from 1778. Three further towers, of a different model, were built from 1807 to 1814, and five others between 1834 and 1837. These precautionary measures were all the more justified since France had become infuriated by the schemes of the Jersey corsairs and had attempted to invade the island on several occasions. A first attempt was made in

Royal Square, where Peirson and Rullecourt's bloody battle took place.

1779 by a powerful fleet led by the Prince of Nassau, a French ally. However, after having crossed the Saint Ouen Bay, in search of a propitious landing site, the fleet was forced into retreat by the island's militia which had been offered sufficient time to gather its spirits, and headed back for Saint Malo.

On a cold January night in 1781, Philippe Macquart, a rather foolhardy French officer, investing himself with the title of Baron of Rullecourt, landed with a troop of mercenaries around the Plate Roque rocks on the island's south coast, despite the natural protection offered by its many reefs. Rullecourt and his men silently slipped their way towards the suburbs of St Helier, taking the Governor Moses Corbet by surprise in his bed, just like his illustrious predecessor Nenfant! Although he signed a declaration of surrender, the alert was rapidly spread. The parish militia and the island's troops gathered together to challenge the invasion, whilst the commander of the Elizabeth Castle garrison refused to acknowledge the capitulation.

Under the command of Major Peirson, a young British officer, the militia reached the town centre and entered Royal Square. Peirson asked the French to surrender. The latter refused. During the subsequent confrontation, Peirson fell at the very first round of fire; however the Jerseyans succeeded in forcing the French out of the town. Rullecourt died a little later from his injuries and the French finally surrendered in the afternoon.

Pub sign bearing the effigy of Major Peirson.

Portrait of Lieutenant (and future
Admiral) Philip Dauvergne, based on a
Jersey postage stamp issued in 1976.

During the French Revolution, the
Comité de Salut Public (Committee
of Public Safety) in turn planned to
invade Jersey, which had become a
refuge for hundreds of emigrants,
among whom Chateaubriand, who
stayed on the island for a few
months, together with several
non-juring priests. However, the
plan was not put into practice. On
the contrary, a French emigrant
army was formed on Jersey and,
on the 3rd of July 1795, sailed to
the Quiberon peninsula where it
was annihilated by Hoche's
revolutionary troops.

Jersey was also one of the
Correspondence bases set up
by the emigrated French
Royalists to ensure the trans-
mission of spies or messages
for the Chouans and
the French Royalist
troops. From the old
Mont Orgueil Castle,
Philip Dauvergne, Duke
and Prince of Bouillon,
was to play the leading role
in coordinating the budding
Royalist intelligence network.
Dauvergne considerably boosted
the Correspondence service, orga-
nising the departure of Royalist
fighters, the delivery of weapons,
and becoming closely involved in
the various attempts at restoring
the monarchy up to the fall of the
Empire. This remarkable figure is
worth a few lines to explain the
events which led to his fortune
and his title.

This young Jerseyman, born in
1754, was a British Navy officer
and the son of a Royal Artillery
captain. Whilst imprisoned in
France, following a shipwreck in
1779, he was fortunate enough to
be noticed by Godefroy de La Tour
d'Auvergne, an extremely wealthy
prince who reigned over the principality of Bouillon, located within
the confines of Luxembourg. The
latter was looking for a successor.
Charmed by Philip Dauvergne, the
prince declared him his heir,
having established, with the help
of genealogists, that the
Dauvergnes from Jersey, settled on
the island since 1232, were in fact a
branch of his own D'Auvergne
family.

Although the duchy was annexed
by the French Republic in October
1795, Philip did not for as much
hesitate to use his title of "Prince",
rushing back to France to claim his
duchy as soon as peace was restored at the Treaty of Amiens in
1802. He was imprisoned in the
Prison du Temple despite his perfectly legitimate papers. His pro-
emigrant activities in Jersey were
well known to the French police
and his past as a British secret
agent – residing in France immediately prior to the Revolution, in
charge of reconnaissance of the
coastal defences – undoubtedly
explains his incarceration. He was
released and expelled seven days
later and returned to Jersey.
Promoted to the grade of Vice
Admiral, but destitute following
costs to recover his principality
which he continued to claim even
after the fall of Napoleon, he died
in 1816, heavily in debt.

Under the French Empire, the fear
of new incursions led to the creation of Fort Regent, on the hill
dominating the town of St Helier;
however such threats were to
considerably diminish following
the annihilation of the French fleet
at Trafalgar in 1805.

Mont-Orgueil, the Prince of Bouillon's Correspondence base.

The 19th Century and the way towards development

The 19th Century was to prove to be a period of economic expansion, despite a few financial disasters. Oyster fishing, which had been the subject of many a clash with the French, the Jerseyans regularly dragging oysters from the French waters, was a particularly lucrative activity. Fishing in Newfoundland flourished once more from 1835 to 1880, certain families, such as the Robins, founding genuine empires. This activity finally disappeared at the end of the century, resulting in the closure of shipbuilding yards. In 1841, the laying of the foundation stone of Victoria harbour in St Helier was to mark a new period in the port's development.

Celebration for the laying of the Victoria Harbour foundation stone (Jersey Museum).

The island's agricultural activities were transformed with the breeding and export of Jersey cows and bulls and the growing of "Royal" potatoes, together with other fruits and vegetables. Although the knitting industry regressed, canvas and linen production remained prosperous.

Jersey Chronicle Almanac, 1892.

The Jersey cow, an excellent dairy cow, is the only breed allowed on the island.

Jersey's railways

St Aubin railway station.

A railway line was created in 1870, linking St Aubin to the island's capital, St Helier. However this narrow 1.06 metre link, run by the Jersey Railway company and stretching as far as the Corbière Lighthouse, was soon to result in St Aubin's economic decline, most of this hitherto prosperous harbour town's activities being transferred to the capital, which now boasted a population of 30,000 inhabitants. A standard, 10 kilometre long, railway line was also opened between 1873 and 1891, linking St Helier to Gorey, and run by the Jersey Eastern Railway. This unprofitable link was to be closed in 1929, whereas the western 14 kilometre long link was in turn to be abandoned in October 1963, following a fire which struck part of St Aubin railway station and a number of wagons. Saint Brelade station was transformed into a parish hall, to house the parish's administrative departments.

The onset of World War I led a great number Jerseyans to enlist as volunteers in the British Army, many of whom perished in the French or Belgian battlefields; however the island of Jersey did not directly suffer from the conflict, contrary to during World War II.

After the French defeat and the Second Armistice in June 1940, the island was demilitarised, just like Guernsey. A small proportion of the population, approximately one fifth and essentially new arrivals, agreed to be evacuated. On the 28th of June, the Luftwaffe bombed the harbour killing 44 islanders. Over and above the dishonour of being under occupation, the Jerseyans were to endure much hardship, along with the iron rule of the Germans whose initial courtesy was but short lived!

The Occupation (photographs displayed at the German Underground Hospital).

During five long years under the enemy's heel, the island's Bailiff, Alexander Coutanche endeavoured to have the islanders' rights respected as far as possible. « I protested », he was later to reply when questioned on what he had done during the Occupation.
He also kept a watchful eye on the difficult preservation of the island's economic activities and on the arrival of fresh supplies.

The German troops, initially 2,000, rapidly increased to 11,500 men, representing 500 occupants for 1 to 3 islanders! In such conditions, defying the enemy proved to be a difficult task. Nevertheless, small ads in Jersey dialect were published in the island's daily newspaper, the Evening Post, although

The Occupant's considerable numbers failed to prevent many acts of resistance (panel displayed in the German Underground Hospital).

under German control, hence bypassing the German censors and transmitting prohibited information received from the BBC via the few radios which had escaped German confiscation in 1942. A total of 2,600 Jerseyans were arrested and imprisoned by the Germans for acts of resistance and 302 were deported to POW camps in France, Germany and Poland.

Entrance to the German Underground Hospital.

With Hitler's order to transform the Channel Islands into impregnable fortresses, huge construction sites were launched in Jersey and a massive influx of several thousands of forced foreign labourers and prisoners arrived on the island. Inland, 16 huge subterranean galleries were planned, aimed at providing shelter for the German garrison. However, less than half of them were actually operational by the end of the Occupation. These tunnels were literally hollowed out of the rock by forced labourers. In St Peter's Valley, they extracted around 44,000 tonnes of rock, in perfectly inhuman conditions, in order to build the immense Ho 8 underground bunker (Hohlgangsanlagen 8), which, although unfinished, was transformed into an underground hospital subsequent to fears of a landing operation. The construction, which had eaten up a total of 6,000m³ of concrete, was initially

German coastal artillery observation tower, Noirmont Point, St Brelade.

Observation post installed in Elizabeth Castle by the Germans.

intended to be used as barracks and artillery store. It was to include 4 large parallel tunnels, 100 metres long and 3 metres wide, linked by 7 smaller tunnels; however, only 2 of the large tunnels were completed.

Anti-tank walls were built along the coastline, the fields were planted with mines and the beaches covered with obstacles. Powerful artillery batteries were built on the heights. By late 1944, there were 37 of such batteries on the island, equipped with 146 guns, without counting the anti-aircraft guns, many of which were installed within the Martello towers.

After the Allied landings in Normandy, the islands found themselves isolated from the free world, surviving only thanks to supplies shipped in by the Swedish ship *Vega*. Following a failed plot against Hitler in February 1945, Jersey's command was entrusted to Vice Admiral Friedrich Hüeffmeier, a committed Nazi. The Vice Admiral, seeking to lead an active resistance campaign rather than simply wait for the war to end, immediately organised a raid on the Norman harbour town of Granville. His aim was as follows: to sabotage ships and the port facilities used for renewing coal supplies, despite the fact that the Allies had already reached the Rhine.

Vice Admiral F. Hüeffmeier inspecting the seamen who took part in the Granville raid (photograph displayed at the German Underground Hospital).

the American and British troops and civilians, along with many wounded, whereas the Germans had only lost six of their men.

After the unfortunate grounding of one of their minesweepers, the Germans finally retreated, taking with them several American prisoners, together with the *Eskwood*, a coaster laden with 116 tonnes of coal, which they towed back to Jersey. The success of the operation reassured the Germans in their plans to organise a similar raid on Cherbourg in April, aimed at hindering the flow of supplies to the front. Thankfully, this second raid failed and the commando was captured by American troops on the 7th and 8th of April, before it had put its plans for destruction into action.

Jersey was finally liberated on the 9th of May 1945.

Over the years following the Liberation, Jersey enjoyed another prosperous period thanks to agriculture and tourism and, as from 1962, as one of the most important international financial centres. In 1972, Jersey, together with its neighbouring isles, decided to boycott the Common Market, preferring to negotiate its own terms.

After nightfall, on the 8th of March, the Granville radar station detected three ships sailing off the coast. This was not immediately considered to be abnormal; however, when at midnight the lookouts noticed that the convoy was approaching Granville, doubt was cast on their intentions. The small French troop posted in the Caserne du Roc barracks was immediately informed. The French soldiers initially supposed that they were facing a military exercise. Hence their great surprise when shellfire started to hit the town and the harbour.

Another raid was simultaneously launched to the north of the Plat-Gousset beach to create a diversion. A German commando landed and gunned down the American officers stationed at the Hôtel des Bains and the Normandy-Hôtel.

However, the harbour remained the Germans' main target. After fierce hand-to-hand combat with the seamen on guard on their ships, the assailants finally managed, by means of explosives, to damage four English cargo ships as well as cranes on the dock. Mines were also placed throughout the town. The attack was to end in the death of twenty people among

The Jersey flag. The only of the islands' flags to bear a St Patrick's cross with Jersey's blazon (3 leopards) surmounted by the Plantagenet crown, in the upper triangle.

Jersey now relies on Portuguese immigrants for agricultural labour.

Today, tourism and finance remain Jersey's main sources of prosperity, representing three quarters of the island's total income. Banks do not fall under the jurisdiction of the United Kingdom and can, therefore, offer their clients highly attractive financial and tax benefits, hence rendering finance and banking the mainstay of the island's economy. Many wealthy immigrants come to Jersey to retire and to shun heavy British taxes.

The islanders are gradually giving up manual professions and the hotel industry to turn to finance and insurance, many new immigrants providing the manpower required to sustain the island's agriculture and tourism. After the influx of Bretons in the 19th Century, to work the land, today's immigrant workers are essentially Portuguese, originating from Madeira or Portugal.

In 2001, they already represented approximately 6.5% of the island's population. Since 2004, the hotel and catering industry has also

Entrance to the States Chamber.

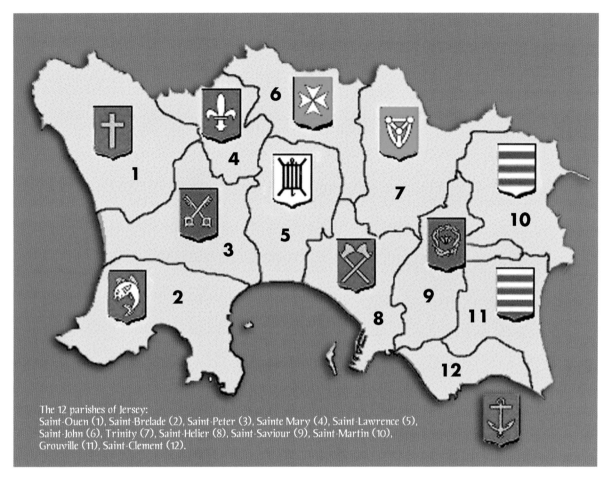

The 12 parishes of Jersey:
Saint-Ouen (1), Saint-Brelade (2), Saint-Peter (3), Sainte Mary (4), Saint-Lawrence (5),
Saint-John (6), Trinity (7), Saint-Helier (8), Saint-Saviour (9), Saint-Martin (10),
Grouville (11), Saint-Clement (12).

attracted manpower from Poland. Nowadays, barely half of the island's inhabitants are original Jerseyans, following the flood of British immigrants, today representing around 35% of the population.

Although Jersey, which is directly answerable to the British Crown, is presided over by a Bailiff, the island has been governed by a Chief Minister since the 5th of December 2005, who coordinates the work of Ministers, in replacement of the former committee system. This system of committees in charge of the island's administration was deemed to be too complex, inadequately efficient and not sufficiently receptive to the voters' opinions. The Bailiff is appointed by the Crown and must be an original

Jerseyan; he/she must also have legal training. He/she simultaneously chairs the States and the Royal Court of justice.

Today, the island's parliament (the States), comprises 53 elected members, a maximum of 23 of whom may simultaneously hold a ministerial position, either as a minister or an assistant minister. The 53 elected members include 12 Senators in office for a period of six years, 29 Deputies in office for three years and 12 Constables, also in office for three years, all of whom are members of the States in reason of their role as parish administrators. Over and above the Bailiff, non-elected members also hold office on the parliament. They are appointed by the Crown; however, they do not have the right to vote. They include the

Lieutenant-Governor, representing the Queen, the Attorney General, the Solicitor General and the Dean of Jersey. In the past, all of the parish rectors were members of the States, similarly to Jurats. The institutional reform of the Channel Islands put an end to this system in 1948.

Any law voted by the States must obtain approval from the Queen's Privy Council. And finally, although Jersey has its own currency and its own postage stamps, the British government remains in charge of its defence and its international relations.

On a local scale, the island is divided into twelve parishes, each of which is administrated by a Constable who chairs a parish assembly dealing with civil affairs.

St Helier and the south coast

The most striking feature when arriving in St Helier is the break created between the town centre and the shoreline by a residential and leisure area encroaching on the sea. The old harbour docks, unlike those in St Peter Port in Guernsey, are now perpendicular to the town, as a result of the creation of new platforms.

and shaded - Royal Square. This is where the monks from the former St Helier priory set up their market, at the very beginnings of the town's creation. It is also the location of the bloody battle which opposed the French and the Jerseyans in 1781, referred to as the "Battle of Jersey" and during which young Major Peirson and the Baron of Rullecourt were mortally wounded. Today this peaceful square is planted with chestnut trees with, in its centre, a statue of King George II, dressed as a Roman emperor, commemorating the generous donation made by the king in 1751 to develop the harbour.

Liberation Square.

Arriving from the harbour, and after having crossed the vast Liberation Square, followed by Mulcaster Street, visitors arrive rapidly at the historical heart of the town; a charming provincial style square, paved

Street names.

Statue of King George II, in Roman emperor dress, Royal Square.

Royal coats of arms on the facade of the Royal Court.

Stone slab engraved in memory of Major Peirson.

On one of the sides of the square stands an imposing granite edifice, built in 1866, and housing the States and the Royal Court. Nearby Royal Square, within a smaller court and the town's former cemetery, stands the 11th Century parish church, enlarged on several occasions and converted into a Calvinist Temple in the 16th Century, during the Civil War. During the Battle of Jersey in 1781, the captured French soldiers were imprisoned in the church.

After having succumbed to his injuries, Major Peirson was buried within the church, in a place of honour opposite the pulpit, where a stone slab has been engraved in his memory.

St Helier parish church.

Vine Street (La Rue des Vignes).

The shopping streets are always busy, even when rain appears imminent.

The impressive States building.

Bath Street, one of St Helier's pedestrian precincts.

At only a stone's throw from Royal Square, the town's trading streets constantly attract crowds of shoppers. Throughout its attractive King and Queen Street, now converted into pedestrian precincts, St Helier is sure to please those partial to a shopping spree whilst enjoying the liveliness of a large town offering an abundant and wide range of retail outlets. St Helier has a multitude of places of interest, but visiting the town by car can prove to be troublesome due to the density of its road traffic.

Town signposting.

The indoor market.

Inside a merchant's house during the Victorian period (Jersey Museum).

Royal Square also leads to the Halkett Place indoor market. Under a high glass roof, dating back to the Victorian period, supported by cylindrical pillars adorned with Corinthian capitals and around a charming fountain, stands an impressive array of superb fruit, flower and vegetable stalls.

Among the town's different museums, too countless all to be mentioned here, the remarkable Jersey Museum is a must. Located within a former 18th Century warehouse, this museum presents the island's past in a particularly attractive and educational manner, and even offers a reconstruction of the La Cotte archaeological site. But it also recounts Jersey's traditions and activities, with a display of beautiful paintings offering an insight into the Jersey landscapes at different periods of its history. Finally, in a merchant's house, contiguous to the former warehouse and accessible from the upper floors, a visit of the interior rooms, precisely as they were around 1860, with their Victorian furniture, is of great interest.

Statue of General Don, Governor of the island from 1806 to 1814, Parade Place park.

Elizabeth Castle artillery battery.

The lower courtyard with a barracks to the right.

Built on a islet off St Helier, Elizabeth Castle is worthy of a lengthy visit to appreciate, not only its maritime site but also its barracks housing permanent exhibitions of particular interest on the role the castle played throughout Jersey's history and of the life of the garrisons who occupied it over the centuries. Nearby, St Helier's Hermitage Rock is accessible via a seawall which also offers access to the small chapel built during the 12th Century in memory of Saint Helier.

Reconstruction of a barrack room.

Hermitage Rock in St Helier, accessible from Elizabeth Castle via a seawall initially intended to extend the harbour.

Entrance to Fort Regent.

is a particularly picturesque harbour town, defended by a fort standing on a rocky islet 500 metres from the shoreline and dating from Henry VIII's reign. On different spots along this coastline, Martello towers were also erected from 1780 to 1814, for example, further west, in the small Portelet Bay, on the Ile au Guerdain or in Saint Brelade Bay, a resort renowned for its fine sandy beach protected by two towers.

Throughout St Aubin's Bay, the German Occupation is still visible to this very day, with anti-tank walls and bunkers, together with two Martello towers. Near the coastal road, St Matthew's church, although not particularly inviting from the outside, offers striking interior glass decoration in Art Nouveau style, created in 1934 by the French artist René Lalique.

To the east of St Helier, the coast is extremely urbanised. Victor Hugo was particularly attached to La Grève d'Azette. Before being expelled to Guernsey, the poet took up residence there for a few years in a house on Marine Terrace.

Approximately 1.5km from the shore, the splendid Samarès Manor, former home to the Samarès family whose descendants, the Saumarez, lived in Guernsey, is located in a magnificent park adorned with a pond.

When arriving in St Helier by sea, the immense white dome covering Fort Regent, so-called in honour of the Prince Regent who became George IV, cannot fail but to catch the eye. The fort, built on a 9 hectare estate on the St Helier heights to enable the inhabitants to seek refuge in the case of an invasion by the Napoleonic troops, was in fact only to be used by the Germans during World War II. Disarmed, the fort has been transformed into a vast leisure and sports centre. It comprises, in particular, an auditorium, a swimming pool, boutiques and cafés.

The south coast boasts many bays, fortified over the centuries, starting with the vast St Aubin's Bay. Located 5 kilometres to the west of St Helier, St Aubin

St Aubin's harbour and bay.

Leisure facilities and attractions inside Fort Regent.

Samarès Manor.

The Japanese garden in Samarès Manor.

Seymour Tower.

This peaceful and inviting place offers pleasant strolls around its rose garden, its aromatic herb garden and its splendid Japanese garden.

On the way back to the coast, but still within the parish of St Clement, lies Le Hocq Point, with its fine Martello tower, then St Clement's Bay, with its "lunar beach", so-called because of the multitude of strange black rocks which emerge at low tide between the sand banks, the small ravines and many sea ponds. A genuine paradise for naturalists, the area abounds with molluscs, shellfish, fish and a multitude of bird species including black and white oystercatchers, grey herons, egrets and even kingfishers.

It was within this very maze of rocks, near La Rocque Harbour, that Baron de Rullecourt and his men succeeded in landing on the island in 1781, facing little resistance. Consequent to this attempted invasion, two defensive towers were erected, one on Plat Roque Point and the other further out to sea, on a reef located 1 mile from the coast. This tower was named Seymour Tower, after the Jersey Governor, General Henry Seymour Conway. La Rocque Point is the southernmost point of the magnificent Royal Bay of Grouville.

Grouville Bay and the east coast

Grouville is an agricultural parish, boasting a magnificent sandy bay, Grouville Bay, to which Queen Victoria added the highly gratifying term "Royal", during her visit to Jersey in 1859. Indeed, this bay forms a perfect curve culminating in the colourful and picturesque facades of Gorey Harbour's houses, surmounted by the daunting mass comprising Gorey Castle. This lovely bay was equipped with 6 Martello towers (one of which has been destroyed) and 2 small forts, Fort Henry and Fort William. Stretches of moorland align the coast and the prestigious Royal Jersey Golf Club occupies the entire coast between the two forts and even a little further to the south.

Mont Orgueil medieval castle, erected on the rock side in the 13th Century and transformed on several occasions up to the 16th Century, is well worth a long visit to discover its many rooms, its courtyards, its towers and its different enclosures, all perfectly restored. The ramparts and the towers offer excellent views of the harbour and the east coast, but also the Ecrehou and even, on a clear day, the Normandy coastline.

On the way northwards, St Catherine's Bay, overlooked by gentle hillocks, stretches from the Archirondel Martello tower, built in 1794 to St Catherine's pier to the north. Construction of this 800 metre long Victorian style pier began in 1847, to be completed in 1855. A second pier was initially planned, starting

St Catherine's pier.

from the Archirondel tower, originally on an islet but linked to the shore at the same time and in the same aim, with a view to creating one of the great naval bases planned for Jersey and Alderney to house a British fleet in the case of French attacks. The development of steam navigation, less vulnerable to poor wind conditions, together with the improved relationship between France and the island rendered these projects obsolete before they were even complete.

The Royal Bay of Grouville.

Mont Orgueil castle with the round tower converted into an observation post by the Germans.

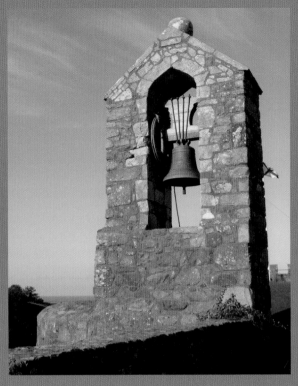

The Governor Sir Thomas Overay's belfry (late 15th Century).

General view of Mont Orgueil Castle.

The 18 metre deep castle well.

St George's Chapel crypt, dating from the 12th Century.

The Queen's Gate, built in 1648 by Sir George Carteret.

14th Century machicolated bastion.

The north and west coasts

Corbiere Lighthouse.

The immense St Ouen's Bay.

To the west of Saint Brelade, after the high La Moye cliffs, an immense chaos of rocks, extended by a series of islets with piercing crests, forms La Corbiere Point. And to ward off vessels from these dangerous reefs, where many a ship has been wrecked, a lighthouse, the first to be built of reinforced concrete, was lit in 1873.

From Corbiere Lighthouse, the immense St Ouen's Bay can be seen stretching across the entire west coast of Jersey, over more than 3km. The bay is renowned for its excellent surfing conditions, since it is exposed to the Atlantic swell. Among the five Martello towers which originally protected the bay, only the Rocco tower built on an isolated rock remains. However, two more recent towers, built between 1835 and 1838 are still visible; the Kempt Tower which now houses an information centre on the

Sark, well visible from Grosnez Castle.

Bouley Bay harbour with the winch from the tug boat *La Mauve'*, dating from 1933 and sunken to form an artificial reef in 1993.

neighbouring natural reserve, and the Lewis Tower. Many vestiges remain of the German Occupation; observation towers, anti-tank walls and bunkers are also scattered across the coastal landscape. A little further inland, marshy ponds now form a natural reserve with a wealth of plant species which have perfectly adapted to this specific environment parti-cularly appreciated by migratory birds.

At the extreme northern tip of St Ouen's Bay, the coastal road rises abruptly, bypassing Les Landes, home to Jersey's race course. To the left, a pathway leads to the desolated promontory referred to as Grosnez Point. This headland is home to the ruins of the former Grosnez Castle, built in local red granite around 1330. Naturally protected on three sides, the castle has a moat on only one of its facades. It offered a precious refuge for the nearby population whenever enemy raids took place, its only weak point being the fact that there was no water supply within the castle walls. Captured by the French in 1373 and again in 1381, it was very probably dismantled during or immediately following the French occupation from 1461 to 1468.

The views from Grosnez Point are magnificent and it is the best place on the island, thanks to its high cliffs, to try to get a glimpse of the islands of Sark, Herm and Guernsey, whilst, nearer the coast at a distance of approximately one and a half miles, the Paternosters (also known as the Pierres de Lecq), responsible for many lost vessels and lives, stand out on the horizon.

The few bays which punctuate from time to time the cliffs on the island's north-west coast, are all worth discove-ring. The Greve de Lecq, accessible via a road travelling through a deep wooded valley, boasts a very popular beach on a sunny summer's day. It was previously defen-ded by a Martello tower, the only one on the north coast still visible today.

Many believe that Bonne Nuit Bay, a charming little fishing port, owes its rather peculiar name to a visit to Jersey by the future King Charles II, who had come to the island during his conflict with the Parliament. The prince is said to have uttered, « Good night beautiful Jersey », before leaving the bay on his way to France. However, in truth, it would appear that mention had already been made of this name, very probably meaning the bay of good rest, in a chart dating from the 12th Century!

Continuing eastwards, the parish of Trinity is not only home to Bouley Bay and its lovely harbour sheltered behind a small jetty, but also to the remarkable Jersey Zoo. Created in 1963 by Gerard Durrell, the zoo is devoted to rare and endangered species. Since Durrell's death, his wife Lee has continued his efforts, along with the Durrell Foundation, also involved in many study programmes on endangered species throughout the world.

Bouley Bay is a natural port which has been used for centuries. In the 17th and 18th Centuries, larger fishing boats were dragged out of the water with the help of capstans. The harbour's development was hindered by the fact that it is situated at the foot of a steep embankment; a jetty was nevertheless built in 1837 when the island's oyster fishing was at its peak. The jetty could welcome up to thirty cutters.

The Black Dog of Bouley

The crystal clear waters around Bouley Bay, although a haven for deep-sea divers, are also reputed to be haunted by the famous Black Dog, a wide-eyed black beast who wreaks terror throughout the area.

« Lé Tchian du Bouôlay 'tait supposé aver sa d'meuthe sus Les Huthets en d'ssus du Bouôlay à La Trinneté (La Trinité), mais ché n'tait pon qu'les Trinnetais tch'en avaient eunne mortelle peux ». That's how the story starts in old Jèrriais, going on to recount how this legendary dog was even seen at night as far as the parish of St Ouen, to the north west of the island! Whenever anyone heard the sound of its chain, because he was said to have « eune grand'chaîne lé tou du co tchi 'tait si longue qu'ou traînait dans ka route dré-the li, » they found themselves paralysed and could no longer move.

Black Dog pub sign.

At the time, liqueur brandies were inexpensive and they were generally not diluted with water! This could well explain, at the end of many a merry evening, certain testimonies from peasants who were rather partial to a dram. Another, more plausible explanation, hinges on the nocturnal activities of smugglers. To compensate for their somewhat mediocre agricultural income, the latter practiced what they referred to as "free trade", importing, without hesitation, clandestine brandy liqueurs from their Cotentin "cousins", under the crown's civil servants' very nose. The Black Dog of Bouley therefore proved to be very useful in discouraging those who may have envisaged some form of nocturnal surveillance!

L'Etacquerel Fort, to the east of Bouley Bay.

Rozel Harbour.

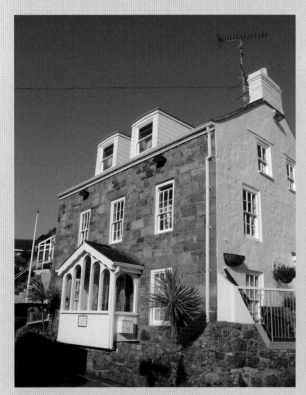

A house in Rozel.

The last bay on the coast, Rozel Bay, shelters a lovely little fishing port, formerly specialised in oyster farming and located in the hollow of a wooded valley bordered with fishermen's houses. It is directly opposite the French village of the same name, on the west coast of the Cotentin peninsula.

English is now the official language; however each place has preserved its French name.

The inland countryside, a maze of small and charming roads.

If Jersey's extremely varied coastline is exceedingly attractive, the same can be said for its inland countryside, revealing a charming and traditional rural habitat, beautiful churches and not forgetting the island's agricultural activities, whilst splendid manor houses stand proud in the heart of its parklands. Although Jersey was home to some 2,600 farms in the last decades of the 19th Century, today, barely 500 remain. Nevertheless, fine herds of Jersey cattle can still be admired, perhaps on a chance encounter along one of the island's extremely narrow yet charming roads whose French names are often reminiscent of their Norman origin.

Among the island's different manor houses, St Ouen's Manor, in the parish of the same name, is steeped in the history of one of Jersey's emblematic families, the Carterets. This fine property is situated within an estate which has belonged to the Carteret family since the feudal period. The present-day manor, requisitio-

St Ouen's Manor.

ned by the Germans during the Occupation and having suffered fire damage in 1941, dates essentially from the 17th Century, but has preserved a lovely door, the former main entrance, dating from the 15th Century.

Saint Mary's Mount, on the way to La Greve de Lecq.

St Ouen's parish church. The early building existed several centuries before William the Conqueror, the church then becoming the pro-priety of the Carteret family who finally donated it to the Mont Saint-Michel abbey.

« Bu de la rue », a traditional Jersey house.

Hamptonne Country Life Museum.

In the parish of St Lawrence, the Hamptonne Country Life Museum brings the island's peasant life back to life throughout its farm buildings, certain of which date back three centuries.

On a totally different note, the remarkable yet tragic museum of the German Occupation, located within the German Underground Hospital, offers a very moving visit as soon as visitors pass the entrance, suggestive itself of a prison or an underground tomb. A successfully designed audiovisual display per-fectly reproduces the period's atmosphere and extremely harsh conditions.

One of the rooms in the German Underground Hospital.

The Ecrehou and the Minquiers, bitterly fought over reefs

The Ecrehou archipelago.

Ecrehou Maîtr'Ile.

In the La Déroute channel, 5 miles from St Catherine's pier on Jersey's most north-easterly point, the vast rocky plateau forming the Ecrehou, administratively part of the parish of St Martin, stretches across a total surface area of over 30km^2 at low tide, whereas only three main islets and a few rocks emerge at high tide.

Maîtr'Ile is a grass-covered mound housing the ruins of a priory. It was built by monks from the Val Richer abbey near Lisieux, after Pierre de Préaux had donated the Ecrehou to them provided that they build a chapel there for masses to be recited in honour of King John, himself and his family.

Maîtr'Ile.

The Ecrehou as seen by Charles Frémine

The Cotentin-born writer Charles Frémine has left us with a very poetic description of the spectacle offered by these reefs at dawn, which, although dating from the 19th Century, is still very faithfull to the scene today, « *All of these granite monsters, of all shapes and sizes, some of them clad up to their wastes in kelp, bald, haggard, whitened with bird droppings, others armoured with shells, plunging their feet into the valleys of fucus, tawny and long-haired like old Gauls, the obscure and the famous, those whose colourful names in fishermen's tales take goodness knows which living or fearsome profiles: L'Etau, Le Moulinier, La Noire, La Plate, Le Trépied, Les Deux-Rousses, La Bigorne, Les Deux-Mamelons, La Pierre-aux-Femmes, Les Dirouilles, all of these stormy athletes, foam chewers and damned from the abyss, in the gentle air, in the dawn that bathes them, seemed to take a new breath, as if weary, blessing the sky for offering them this moment's respite, doleful, resigned, ready for new combat* ».

Granite monsters clad with kelp.

Marmotière at high tide.

Marmotière and Blanche-Ile are linked, except at high tide, by a magnificent bed of pebbles.

On La Marmotière, 500 metres further north, fifteen houses are cramped side by side, due to the island's extreme exiguity. On spring tides, the island barely covers 10 ares (a thousand square metres)!

There are also a few houses on La Blanche Ile, which is separated from La Marmotière at high tide, but linked to the latter at low tide by a 100 metre long bed of pebbles.

There is no shelter around these islands in the case of stormy weather. Consequently the Ecrehou can only be reached when weather conditions are favourable. It is possible to berth to the west of La Marmotière, in a small pond which guarantees a level of 1.2 metres even at low tide.

From 1846 to 1898, Philippe Pinel, the first « King of the Ecrehou » lived on La Blanche Ile with his wife, until she returned to Jersey, tired of being beaten by her, often inebriated, husband. Charles Frémine met with Philippe Pinel during an excursion to the Ecrehou, « *A genuine savage, that one, and who was one step ahead of my dream. His small and henceforth unseaworthy craft lay, the hull overturned, a few steps from his pebbled cabin. Giant mallows, the only plants capable of growing on Blanque-Ile, swathed it with their high blossom-less shafts. And they covered, with their pale curtain, the loner's hermitage.* »

In the 1960's, another Jerseyman, Alphonse Legastelois, whose parents were originally from Manche in France, was regarded by the locals as a marginal character and, as such, was wrongly accused of abuse inflicted in the moorlands on the island's women and children. Failing proof, he was freed and, both fearing for his life and following a fire in his home, he left Jersey in 1967 to settle on La Marmotière.

Then Alphonse, the new King of the Ecrehou, hated by the Jerseyans who had wrongly taken him for a criminal, pronounced the Clameur de Haro before two witnesses, claiming the ownership of the island from the Queen. His claim was based on the Norman right which clearly states that any permanently uninhabited territory may become the propriety of he who regularly resides there for a period of ten years. However, Alphonse Legastelois' request was rejected. The genuine perpetrator of the aggressions was finally arrested in 1971. However Alphonse did not give up on his island! A few years later, following incidents on La Marmotière, and taking advantage of an official rat and rabbit extermination operation, the States of Jersey obliged Alphonse to return to Jersey where they paid him a small pension.

Jersey's coat of arms as seen on the tax office on Marmotière, asserting Jersey's sovereignty.

The Ecrehou, only inhabited a few days each year by British citizens, have been more often than not deserted, with the exception of the two aforementioned and short-lived "royalties", and were generally used as hideouts by smugglers who hid fabric, carrots of tobacco and casks of alcohol on their travels between the isles and the Cotentin peninsula. Their territoriality has nevertheless been bitterly, and for a long time, disputed.

A little step back in time will help us to appreciate the ever-present French interest in the Ecrehou. Following the fall of the French Empire, the neighbouring Granville oyster beds, initially only exploited by French fishermen, began to attract the Jersey fishermen who had previously contented themselves with the waters around their own island. Despite an initial agreement concluded in 1824, Jersey's fishermen continued to drag in the French waters, including the shores before Régneville and in the La Déroute channel. Tension was on the increase, along with the number of incidents. New negotiations were launched between the British and French authorities, leading to a fishing agreement in 1839, delimiting the zones belonging to each country, along with a neutral zone including the Ecrehou and the Minquiers, situated 8 miles south of Jersey.

In the summer, the Jersey flag flies on the tiny square before Marmotière's few houses.

In 1875, the French Naval Ministry was concerned about the recent claim laid by the Jersey authorities pertaining to their rightful possession of the Ecrehou. Indeed, the establishment of British batteries on the islands' peaks had put a stop to any possible navigation between the rocks and the French coast, also blocking the La Déroute channel. Finally, this appropriation of the archipelago was to upset the fishing agreements concluded with difficulty in 1839 between the French and the Jerseyans.

Many boats from Carteret, Portbail, Diélette and Granville regularly fished in the waters around the Ecrehou, finding shelter, when necessary, in a natural harbour to the east of Maîtr'Ile.

the Ecrehou is a certain distance from the frontier with the French territorial waters. And their claim to the Minquiers, located even further from the French coast, was in their opinion all the more justified!

The Minquiers stand 12 miles to the south of Jersey and 8 miles to the north-west of the Chausey Islands, comprising a vast plateau of emerging rocks and a multitude of tiny islets. Low tide reveals immense white sandy beaches and islets bordered by streams stretching across a foreshore of around 300km^3. Indeed, the tides here can reach an amplitude of up to 14 metres! At high tide, twenty or so rocks loom up out of the waters, whilst Maîtr'Ile, 150 metres long by 40 metres large, is literally swept by the sea in stormy winds, ren-

Today's anchorages around Marmotière.

France consequently officially protested on the 17th of February 1876, via its ambassador in London. However, this was not to prevent the Jerseyans from maintaining their position and from Great Britain to replying, on the 12th of July 1876, that the Ecrehou comprised a historical propriety upon which the Jersey authorities had established their jurisdiction over several centuries.

The Jerseyans believed their claim to be perfectly justified, all the more so since the 3 mile limit to the east of

At low tide, vast stretches of sand and rocks appear around the Minquiers' Maîtr'Ile.

The Minquiers' Maîtr'Ile.

dering any human settlement on the island totally impossible. However, surprisingly, a few fishing cabins have survived there, today transformed into makeshift refuges for enthusiasts from Jersey keen on such wild and deserted locations. The three leopard Jersey coat of arms, the *"treis cats"*, with *"Impôts"* (taxes) engraved on one of the small houses reminds us that, just like the Ecrehou, this windswept archipelago is also part of the Bailiwick of Jersey.

In the early 1830's, a sounding campaign was launched by the French to distinguish the Minquiers plateau. The Jerseyans were moved by this initiative. However, if truth be told, they paid little attention to these waters, contrary to the French, whose ships were obliged to bypass this vast archipelago when sailing from the north-west on their way to Saint-Malo and Granville. In poor weather conditions, in fog or at night, many ships were lost there.

Thus, during the winter of 1861-1862, the Granville-based brig La Marie was lost, together with its 54-man crew, on its way home from Saint Pierre and Miquelon. Then, on the 12th of January, the brig Les Trois Frères, was shipwrecked on its way back from the Isle of Rhé,

with the loss of eleven seamen. The Granville Town Council, supported by the Chamber of Commerce, requested that lights be installed on the Minquiers. On the 25th of December 1865, a French light-ship was put into service on the plateau's south-west point. It was replaced, late 1891, by a system of illuminated buoys located around the archipelago.

In 1867, a new fishing agreement was ratified by both France and Great Britain; however it was not respected and incidents between fishermen from both nations continued. In 1890, Britain proclaimed its sovereignty over the Minquiers, and France failed to react. Nevertheless, as soon as the British hoisted the Union Jack on the Minquiers, the French protested via its diplomatic network.

In 1932, Edouard Leroux, a Parisian banker originally from Agon, obtained a lease from the *Administration des Domaines* (French Property Operations Administration) to build a house on the Minquiers. Facing the great agitation the affair provoked in Jersey, and whilst the walls of the house had already reached a height of 4 metres, the Manche Préfet had the lease annulled.

The Minquiers archipelago.

Six years later, the President of the Council, Edouard Daladier, together with Admiral Darlan and several ministers, visited the Minquiers to check the state of the buoys which continued to be maintained by France.

Préfet addressed to Marin-Marie, enjoining him to stop the construction. However, since the shelter was already complete, the members of the expedition continued to work on its interior, hanging a portrait

Fishermen's houses on Maîtr'Ile.

In 1939, Marin-Marie Durand de Saint-Front, a painter and world famous yachtsman thanks to his solitary Atlantic sailboat crossing in 1933, only the second Frenchman to have succeeded such a feat, secretly organised an expedition to the Minquiers with companions from Granville and the Chausey Islands. To assert the French rights and to thwart the Jerseyans' fervent claims on the site, Marin-Marie and his friends established a refuge cabin for the many fishermen from Chausey and Granville who regularly sailed around this perilous archipelago.

Discovering the work that was underway, the Jerseyans alerted the French authorities and, on the second day of construction work, a French hydroplane flew repeatedly over the area. The pilot finally had a weighted message dropped from the Naval

of the President of the French Republic and raising their glasses to the success of their venture.

During the Occupation, a small Kriegsmarine detachment was posted on the Minquiers. And on the 27th of May 1945, the British flag was once more hoisted on Maîtr'Ile. On the 10th of July, Counter-Admiral Graziani, the Naval Préfet, in turn had a flag pole erected, opposite the British flag. The flag pole was sawn down in August and had to be replaced. The French Foreign Affairs Minister then obtained from the Foreign Office the guarantee that the status quo would be maintained and that the French fishermen's cabin would not be vandalised by the Jerseyans.

To put a permanent end to the quarrel, both nations decided in 1953, after having negotiated a new fishing agreement to preserve their respective rights, to bring their dispute before the International Court of Justice in The Hague. After having heard both parties, the court judged in favour of the United Kingdom. Marie-Marin's cabin was therefore demolished and a

The Jersey authorities were far from amused by this "literary prank", all the more so since it was, in fact, subsequent to a similar operation conducted in 1984 upon Jean Raspail's own initiative; however the British

A helicopter landing pad has replaced Marin-Marie's refuge cabin.

helicopter landing pad created on the same spot. However, the French are not likely to forget those deserted islands.

"On Sunday the 30th of April 1998, at dawn a light naval division belonging to the Patagonian Fleet landed on the formerly British archipelago of the Minquiers... This operation, an initiative of the government of His Majesty Orelie-Antoine I, King of Patagonia, aims at reclaiming the sovereignty of his kingdom over the Minquiers colony," stated a press release from the Patagonian Consulate General. Jean Raspail and his many friends recall this fleeting kingdom in his great works, « I, Antoine de Tounens, King of Patagonia ». The Patagonian flag, with its horizontal blue white and green stripes, replaced the Union Jack on the Minquiers, the latter, according to Raspail, "may be returned with honour to Her Majesty's British Embassy in Paris".

authorities kept their stiff upper lip and Jean Raspail, at the time Patagonia's Consulate General in France, returned the Union Jack captured by the second commando to the British Embassy in Paris with dignity, stating nevertheless, as reported in the Daily Telegraph's 2nd of September 1998 issue,
« I cannot guarantee that the Patagonian flag will never be hoisted once more, perhaps a long time after my death. This is but the beginning of a long tradition ».

Simultaneously, far from the French capital, and a few 18 miles from the Cotentin coastline, the immense plateau of the Minquiers, a land of dreams and of nightmares alike, continues to emerge on the surface of the water at each tide, in an eternal and unchanging rhythm, to the delight of its sole permanent inhabitants; gulls, cormorants, Northern gannets, seals and dolphins, each and every one of them oblivious to such human quarrels.

Mont Saint-Michel bay as seen from Saint-Jean-le-Thomas.

The Cotentin islands,

from west to east

Nature and history have transformed the Mont Saint-Michel bay into an exceptional and magnificent site. The bay forms a vast circular arch opening out into the English Channel to the north-west, with an infinite foreshore stretching across 200km² and whose uniformity is broken only by the granite islets of the Mont Saint-Michel and Tombelaine. As Gustave Flaubert described, « *it appears like a desert from which the sea has retreated* ». Given the range of over 15 metres during equinoctial tides, the Mont Saint-Michel's tides rank in third position across the globe after the Bay of Fundy in Canada and the Severn Estuary in England.

The Mont Saint-Michel and Tombelaine.

The Mont Saint-Michel and Tombelaine

Although perfectly visible from the Mont Saint-Michel or the Champeaux cliffs, the islet of Tombelaine remains swathed in mystery. Abandoned by man and difficult to reach, Tombelaine stands high amidst the bay's sands, at 2.8 kilometres from the Mont Saint-Michel. With a surface area of around 4 hectares, this deserted islet may be larger than the Mont Saint-Michel, but its highest summit, the Pic de la Folie, only reaches 45 metres.

Tombelaine.

have been given to the smaller mount nearby.

According to legend, during the first centuries of our era, the Mont Saint-Michel and Tombelaine were surrounded by a dense forest, the forest of Sissy.

The truth, although quite different, is no less incredible! Around 20,000 years ago, the last ice age was at its peak and the sea level was 120 metres below the present day level. At the time, the bay was a valley scoured by violent winds

Since then, silt and sediment have begun to obstruct the site, the incoming currents, stronger than the ebbing tide, bringing with them masses of residue.

In 1048, Anastase, one of the monks from the Mont Saint-Michel, along with a second monk, Robert, decided to retire to the deserted islet of Tombelaine. The two monks built a modest chapel on this site propitious to contemplative life.

In the 12th Century, a priory developed and people from the coast came to build houses, whilst the first pilgrims rushed to the islet to pray Notre-Dame-de-Tombelaine, on their way to the Mont. Pilgrimages were frequent up to the Hundred Years' War which was to seriously disturb their continuation.

After landing in Saint-Vaast in July 1346, King Edward III of England sent troops to attack different Norman strongholds including the Avranchin district. Tombelaine was victim to a surprise siege. From then on, the rock was to be a constant subject of dispute between France and England, both nations successively occupying it. In 1372, the English made incursion onto Tombelaine, but the islet was rapidly retrieved. Reconquered in 1418, again by the English, the tiny stronghold was recovered once more, a few months later, by knights from the Mont Saint-Michel. In 1423, the English captured the islet once more and fortified it, building stronger walls. They were even better protected against incursions by the defenders of the Mont,

Popular tradition attributes the islet's name to the tragic story of Helena, the niece of a Breton king, captured by a giant and taken by force to the islet where she committed suicide after having suffered abused. A more plausible explanation is that the name is simply derived from the Mont Saint-Michel's primitive name, "Mont Tumba" (tomb). The diminutive Tumbellana is thought to

and subjected to an almost Arctic climate. When the earth began to warm, the sea gradually rose, flooding the English Channel.

By around 9000 years BC, the sea had reached approximately 30 metres below today's level. Then around 6000 years BC, the bay was formed due to the continuing rise in the sea level which had reached the present-day town of Pontorson, now situated 7 kilometres inland.

which was still in French hands, following the shift of the bed of the River Couesnon which, from 1420 onwards, passed between the Mont and Tombelaine, forming a natural obstacle which proved difficult to cross.

On the 17th of June 1434, the English, who had encircled the Mont Saint-Michel with a series of small forts, decided once more to launch an assault which they hoped, this time, to conclude. However the Count of Suffolk and Lord Thomas of Scale's troops failed to open sufficient breaches in the Mont's ramparts. Following several hours of combat, Louis d'Estouville and the Mont's knights even succeeded in pursuing the English who retreated towards the shore and in recovering consequential spoils including two large cannons, visible to this day, in the first courtyard at the Mont's entrance.

Nevertheless, Tombelaine remained English up to mid-May 1450, when its occupants finally accepted an "honourable" surrender after having been besieged by Duke François de Bretagne and Constable de Richmont's knights and men-at-arms.

At the end of the 15th Century, Tombelaine and the Mont Saint-Michel saw their military importance considerably diminish. In 1646, the young King Louis XIV had Tombelaine's garrison removed, abandoning the stronghold and,

The course of the River Couesnon, after having fluctuated over time, finally attributed the Mont to the region of Normandy.

English artillery recovered in 1434 by the Mont's defenders.

Statue of St Michael,
Mont Saint-Michel church.

at the time belonged to the Mont Saint-Michel, was confiscated, just like all of the other clergy possessions. The Mayor of Genêts bought the island and had a small guardroom built for the watchmen in charge of observing and transmitting maritime signals from Cherbourg to Brest.

In the heart of the sand bank, at a distance of 1.5 miles from Tombelaine, stands another large and, at the very least, extraordinary rock rising 80 metres above the sand. The Mont Saint-Michel, just like Tombelaine or, further inland, Mont Dol, is an extremely hard granite islet which has succeeded in resisting the natural erosion which has smoothed away the rest of the bay which essentially comprised more fragile shale.

In the early 13th Century, whilst the worship of St Michael had begun to spread throughout Europe, the Archangel Michael, as legend would have it, appeared three times before Aubert, Bishop of Avranches, and ordered him to found a sanctuary in his honour on Mont-Tombe, the Mont Saint-Michel's early name.

To convince Aubert, who was rather sceptical about this supernatural communication, the irritated Archangel touched the bishop's head with his finger, leaving a hole in the skull of the unbeliever. The bishop therefore hesitated no further and had a small chapel in the form of a grotto built at the foot of the Mont, establishing a college of twelve canons there. The first pilgrims arrived.

Under the Norman dukes, the canons were replaced in 966 by Benedictine monks who built the preromanesque church known as Notre-Dame-sous-Terre and upon which the abbey-church nave was to be built as from 1023. When they were not in prayer, the Mont's monks copied and illuminated manuscripts covering a diversity of subjects. The abbey, whose scriptorium was renowned as early as the 11th Century, was to be of considerable intellectual influence.

hence, enabling Jacques de Montgomery, Sire of Lorges, to use the site to produce counterfeit coins and to store weapons and ammunition. Wanted by the king and hunted for over ten years, he was finally captured and sent to the Bastille.

Demolition of the stronghold began in February 1666. The islet was henceforth completely deserted. Twenty-four years later, Louis XIV accepted a petition from the monks and inhabitants of the Mont Saint-Michel requesting that the gates of the Tombelaine fortress, which had been kept, be given to replace the Mont Saint-Michel town gates, which were in a poor state.
Tombelaine and its remaining ruins then fell into oblivion. During the French Revolution, the islet, which

The cloister, suspended between the sky and the sea.

In the 12th Century, the Anglo-Norman kingdom reached its peak at the same time as the Mont thanks to the very good terms between Henry II Plantagenet and the Abbot Robert de Torigny. The monastery was to experience a period of not only spiritual but also temporal development.

The Mont Saint-Michel and its famous salt meadow lamb.

After the Conquest of Normandy, the King of France, Philip Augustus offered donations to the abbey in compensation for damage caused by his Breton allies who had set fire to the Mont. These donations allowed for La Merveille to be built, a Gothic monastery whose construction was undertaken by Abbot Raoul Desisles. During the same period, the first stone enclosure was built around the village at the foot of the abbey.

La Merveille is an exceptional architectural achievement comprising two 3-level buildings supported by huge buttresses. The first floor houses the striking *salle des hôtes* (hosts' room), together with the knights' room, which is in fact the scriptorium. The cloister crowns these two rooms, as if suspended between the sky and the sea, communicating with both the refectory and the abbey-church. This outstanding architecture was intended to please God and the monks and pilgrims who also contributed, by means of offerings, to the monastery's prosperity. Up

The Mont, protected by its ramparts, resisted against the many English attacks during the Hundred Years' War.

to the 18th Century, the Mont was among the world's major pilgrimage destinations alongside Rome and Santiago de Compostela.

However, the abbey did not escape the tribulations of temporal life. During the Hundred Years' War, the Mont Saint-Michel, whose curtain of ramparts and towers had been reinforced, was besieged, as we have already noted, on several occasions by the English. Furthermore, the English, in possession of Tombelaine, taxed the pilgrims wishing to travel on towards the Mont Saint-Michel. Finally, the Mont remained the only French fortification in

Normandy, despite the fact that its Abbot, Robert Jolivet, had sided with the English.

The successive abbots who followed the Hundred Years' War only rarely came to the Mont, hence generating a certain disregard of monastic rules. The buildings were no longer maintained and by the late 16th Century, certain monks even lived with wives and children. The arrival of the Benedictines of the Congregation of Saint Maur was to curb this decline for a while; however by the end of the 18th Century, there were only a dozen or so monks who were finally forced from the "Free Mont" by the French Revolutionary troops.

The Gabriel Tower.

Already a monastery and a fortification, the Mont Saint-Michel was also to serve as a prison. A simple place of detention for a few political prisoners under the Ancien Régime, the Mont was to become a genuine prison during the French Revolution.

Several non-juring priests were incarcerated there as from 1793. Being afforded the official status of State prison in 1811, the Mont Saint-Michel received hundreds of common law detainees as well as political detainees after the 1830 and 1838 revolutions.

The Mont or the La Merveille battery was armed on several occasions. This precautionary measure appeared no longer to be a necessity since the garrison required to control the 700 to 800 detainees was perfectly sufficient to ward off any attempted raid.

Victor Hugo visited the Mont Saint-Michel in 1836 and rebelled against the abbey prison in a letter addressed to his wife, « *Imagine a prison, that intangible yet deformed and fetid thing referred to as a prison, set up within this magnificent envelope of 14th Century priests and knights. A toad in a reliquary. When will, in France, the saintliness of monuments be at last implicit? ...In the castle, all is but noise of locks, noise of labour, shadows watching over shadows working (for a meagre twenty-five sous per week), spectres in old rags shifting in the pallid darkness under the ancient monks' arches, the admirable knights' room, become a workshop where, through a small window, hideous and grey men can be seen bustling... »*

Napoleon III had the prison closed in 1863. The abbey and the village were listed as Historical Monuments in 1874.

Fifty-two years later, in 1926, the bay was the scene of much agita-

In 1836, Victor Hugo rebelled against the abbey prison.

tion. Tombelaine was in the spotlight once more with a major tourist development project focusing on the construction of a large hotel on the islet, including a 200 metre long patio and a church whose spire was to rival that of the neighbouring Mont. This utopic project was to end, six years later, in the bankruptcy of the *Groupement National de la Baie du Mont Saint-Michel*, which had been created to ensure its management and the recovery of the islet by the French State. More recently, in October 1985, an ornithological reserve was created on the islet of Tombelaine which welcomes little egrets and gulls.

From now on, whilst major work is underway to dredge the bay, only hoards of passive walkers haunt this coast and its vast and infinite landscape of intermin-

gling sea and sand, forming, with Tombelaine and the Mont Saint-Michel, and ever-changing panorama. Since 2001, two new monk and cloistered nun communities, living within the abbey, offer daily praise and monastic hospitality, restoring the age-old traditions of meditation and generosity.

The Mont and its bay, a symphony of colours.

Chausey, a labyrinthine archipelago

The Chausey archipelago, through which the Sound runs.

The tiny archipelago of Chausey, located 8.5 miles from Granville, offers visitors a marvellous sight. Abundant islands and islets stretch across over 5,000 hectares at low tide, thanks to a huge tidal amplitude: 14.50 metres! At high tide, the fifty or so islets which remain visible and cover a total surface area of only 75 hectares, form a genuine maritime labyrinth reuniting a multitude of navigable corridors and rocks which are not to be dared.

Grande Ile is a rock measuring 1,800 metres long by a range of 200 to 700 metres wide, and covering a surface area of 45 hectares. Undulating and covered with trees, Grande Ile combines landscapes so truthfully portrayed by Gilbert Hurel, a keen enthusiast, as, *"minute country landscapes clinging to a tumult of granite"*: hollow paths reminiscent of the Normandy bocage, broom and gorse covered heaths and small white houses bordered by pinasters, palm trees and rockeries. Opposite Grande Ile, the Sound offers a very popular deep-water anchorage, particularly pleasant at low tide, since protected from most of the local winds.

When leaving the wooden wharf or the landing slipway, a long and discreet white barrier can be seen, separating the island into two, unequal parts. The smallest part, housing the lighthouse, the fort, the hotel and a few holiday homes, belongs to the State. The other part of the island, covering 39 hectares, together with the archipelago's other islands, belongs to the *Société Civile Immobilière des Iles Chausey*, which inherited from three centuries of successive proprietors. Indeed, after Louis XV declared Chausey as royal property, the Crown only

The lighthouse and the State-owned estate.

actually held onto the archipelago for thirty-five years.

The Société Civile Immobilière des Iles Chausey allows free visits to its property. Finally, Chausey is administratively governed by the town of Granville.

The first signs of human settlement in the archipelago date back to the Megalithic period: a dolmen near the Grande Ile chapel, funerary chambers on the Genétaie islet to the north-west of Grande Ile and a cromlech, 12 metres in diameter, to the north of the islet of Grand Colombier, situated opposite Grande Ile, on the other side of the Sound.

Over the centuries, these rocks have been the subject of many a determined battle for supremacy. In 1022, Richard II, Duke of Normandy, donated the Chausey Islands to the Mont Saint-Michel abbots; however the latter gradually lost interest in the islands following too frequent incursions by Jerseyans, British troops and a great number of rather disreputable seamen. A few fishermen and quarrymen settled on the islands in the late 11th Century. Hence began a long period of Chausey granite extraction.

Contrary to Granville, whose cliffs are of schist, Chausey is entirely composed of red, grey or blue granite.

The Benedictines, followed by the Franciscans, retired there for a while to, in turn, become wearied by the many acts of violence, finally abandoning the archipelago at the onset of the Hundred Years' War. After the English had left the Cotentin, the Franciscans returned to Chausey. However their monastery was twice pillaged by the English in 1543. To prevent the still too frequent incursions, a garrison of 60 men was posted on Grande Ile and a fort was built in 1559.

On the 27th of April 1694, the English made a further forced landing on Chausey, again pillaging

The Chausey Sound.

Château Renault has replaced the old fort.

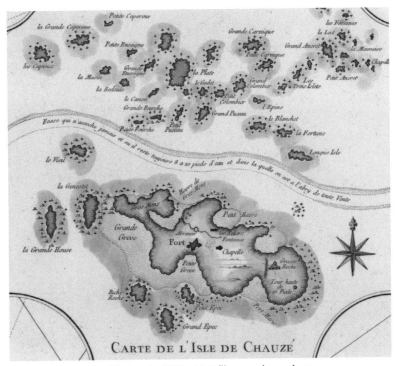

CARTE DE L'ISLE DE CHAUZÉ

Map of the Chausey archipelago in 1757 by M. Bellin, a marine engineer.

Small fishing boats with the former semaphore in the background.

the island, where only Monsieur de Matignon, the governor's farmer and eight quarry employees were present. They dismantled the fort and even threatened to burn the farmer's house. And the following year, they came back to do likewise! The French garrison, which only comprised five men, had no choice but to surrender, after having attempted a few bursts of cannon fire and musket shots.

At a time when smuggling was increasingly widespread within the Channel Islands, Chausey and the Cotentin coastline, a guard post, built in 1737 upon an initiative by the *Fermiers Généraux* (farmers general) on the site of the former fort, was burned down in 1744 by two corsairs from Jersey. They met with no resistance, the archipelago having been, once more, deserted after war had been declared. But Chausey was not to remain deserted for long, with the arrival of 400 labourers from the Channel

Islands, to extract stone for export to Jersey, Guernsey and Alderney. However, it was only when peace was restored in 1748 that the intruders were finally ousted out and the six employees of the Fermes cutter reoccupied the archipelago.

In 1755, smugglers attacked the *Fermes* cutter in the archipelago's waters, massacring three of its crew members. This tragic incident could but reinforce the necessity to establish a fort on Grande Ile. Whilst hostilities were anew, construction of a redoubt was underway in 1756. A small English squadron immediately invaded Chausey and forced the island's garrison into surrender.
The garrison was taken back to Granville with forty or so labourers from the islands; the English were then free to destroy the new fort and plunder the houses and the quarries.
Keen to reaffirm its sovereignty over the archipelago once peace

had been restored, the royal powers had a guard post built for the *Fermes* employees, upon the initiative of Captain Régnier who had settled in Chausey to produce soda ash.

On the 10th of December 1778, the king's corvette, the *Guêpe*, whilst hunting out an English corsair, noticed a great number of men and women apparently distraught at having been discovered by the corvette's captain. The latter had a small boat armed and the vessel's crew was soon face to face with several French women and a dozen Jerseymen who promptly sought refuge in their small cutter, anchored between the rocks.
Sire Régnier's home was subsequently searched and a huge stock of smuggled clothing was seized. If truth be told, such commerce was tolerated by the French authorities since it enabled them to obtain information on the situation in Jersey!

Over the centuries, Chausey's granite was increasingly sought after, be it for work on the Mont Saint-Michel, for Granville's houses and quays, without forgetting the Saint-Malo ramparts or even, as already mentioned, to satisfy the needs of Jersey or the English islands themselves! In the 19th Century, 37 of Chausey's islets were inhabited and several hundreds of quarrymen, now from Brittany and the Cotentin, had settled in dilapidated thatched cottages to work there. From dawn to dusk, they extracted, trimmed and cut, up to their knees in sludge or in water. Then large rowing boats of around 8 metres in length, referred to as *Coucous*, equipped with a square well in the centre surmounted by a winch, loaded each block of granite with the ebbing tide by positioning themselves immediately above, then warped their cargo of over tonnes towards the coasters which were to transport the granite.

From the 17th to the 19th Century, *barrilleurs* (literally coopers), so-called since they shipped their production by means of barrels, were also very active in and around Chausey. Originally from the village of Blainville, near Coutances, they settled on the islands to produce soda ash, by burning kelp in stoves put together at ground level, after having cut and sun-dried the algae. Their cabins, situated near to a sheltered cove overlooking the Sound, provided the foundations of what was to become the village of Les Blainvillais. Originally only simple shelters covered with a web of branches and broom, the village was renovated upon the initiative of the industrialist, Louis Renault. In 1840, the islands' soda ash production had reached 350 tonnes, occupying some 30 men. By 1870, 300 tonnes were still produced.

The fort in 1866.

In 1845, a lighthouse was built on a square tower with a central freestone building. Its light, of a range of 23 miles, has since been automated and its crystal white glare sweeps the archipelago every five seconds. In 1866, the construction of a fort on Grande Ile was finally complete. This pentagonal casemate fort is surrounded by 15 metre large dry ditches, hollowed out from the granite face. Contrary to its predecessors which, barely had they been built, were destroyed by the English, this new fort, although relegated forty years after its construction due to advances in weaponry, still stands today and its bunkers now welcome fishermen.

In the vicinity of the lovely Port Homard beach, this former fort abandoned in the 19th Century, was rebaptised Château Renault in 1923 by the famous automobile industrialist Louis Renault, charmed by Chausey's austere beauty. The present-day chapel, built in 1848 and following a former edifice depicted on a map dating from 1757, offers further evidence of the island's abundant population during the 19th Century. However, this population was to dissipate during the following century.

The village of Les Blainvillais.

Grande Ile is particularly popular during the summer months.

Grande Ile was only permanently inhabited, as from 1970, by around fifteen fishing families. Chausey's last priest, Abbot Delaby, who was as talented at repairing boat engines as he was souls, left the island in 1981, whereas the school had already been closed in 1972. The former farm finally ceased its production in 1989, following the retirement of its farmers, and has since been converted into rented holiday homes.

Today, the archipelago is practically deserted during the winter months, welcoming only a few fishermen and oyster farmers. Equally, in the summer, the island of Chausey is bubbling with excitement with its ever-increasing influx of tourists taking advantage of a day-trip via the ferries linking Grande Ile to the mainland, along with the many Norman, Breton and English sailing enthusiasts who come to land there.

This daily summer ebb and flow could well threaten the natural balance of the archipelago, which remains one of the English Channel's most remarkable natural sites. Fishing enthusiasts can still find lobster, prawns conger eel or sea bass, but for how long? The rich and diverse seabed offers abundant nourishment for the islands' fauna. Porpoises, razorbills and guillemots can sometimes be seen whilst Northern gannets, cormorants, oystercatchers and many other bird species such as common shellducks also take full advantage of the riches the sea has to offer there. This exceptional environment is no less fragile and its preservation is vital.

Mussel bed on Chausey.

$\mathcal{P}$elee Island, a fortress in the Cherbourg roadstead

Mazes of high and murky corridors, vaulted and clammy with dampness; on the ground lie rails upon which wagons no longer run and, occasionally, in the odd gallery, rusty pieces of scrap iron or a devastated tie bed, stairs appearing to lead to nowhere... we are within the antrum of the fort of Pelee Island. This fort, which occupies the entire island and whose exterior architecture remains remarkable, despite the fact that it has been partly demolished and concreted up, also houses particularly sinister internal galleries, abandoned since the Liberation.

Interior gallery in Pelee island fort.

Pelee Island is situated 3 kilometres from the shores of Tourlaville and, according to local tradition, up to the 17th Century fishermen from the coast could reach the island by foot. In the 17th Century, the island was exploited by skippers who came to collect kelp which they in turn burned to produce soda ash. However, in the 18th Century, given its location, this rather low rock was to prove to be of strategic interest to the town of Cherbourg. Indeed, the Cherbourg bay had been selected for the establishment of a major naval port, an asset which was seriously lacking in the Manche County. As we know, the English had destroyed Cherbourg's only merchant port following their incursion and subsequent occupation in 1758.

Among the two opposing development options, the Naval officers' preferred project was finally selected, involving the creation of a high sea roadstead capable of sheltering an entire fleet of ships of the line. The choice was made despite opposition from military engineers and from Dumouriez, the Cherbourg stronghold's new commander, who had envisaged a simple military port reinforced by an arsenal, far easier to defend than a vast stretch of water. In 1783, La Bretonnière, the harbour's designer, together with the French Navy, obtained that work begin with the roadstead's closing seawall.

However, in 1779, before the decision had even been made, the king's cabinet had already ordered that a fort be erected on Pelee Island, following plans drawn up by the civil engineer, Pierre-Jean de Caux. A few years later, the seawall construction work was launched and a first wooden cone, designed to be ballasted to form the foundations of the seawall, was sunk on the 6th of June 1784 after having been towed to the appropriate spot. During the same year, Pelee Island fort, which had been under construction for six years, was finally complete.

Similarly to the other forts built afterwards, Pelee Island fort, which flanks the channel to the east, was originally arranged around a central courtyard. Pierre-Jean de Caux, director of the Lower Normandy fortifications, took the Marquis de

Access ramp leading to Pelee Island fort.

Pelee Island fort seen from Grande Rade.

Montalembert's observations into account, the latter having come to Cherbourg in 1777 and being renowned for his innovative fortification design.

Without for as much transforming the fort into a group of cannon towers, as suggested by Montalembert, Pierre-Jean de Caux nevertheless altered his initial plans by replacing its angular outline by rounder forms, less vulnerable to warship fire, and by having their firing power reinforced.

Equipped with two floors of casemate artillery batteries, surmounted by a terrace roof housing a further battery which was protected by a crenulated parapet, the fort,

The Cherbourg roadstead and Pelee Island in 1833.

already in service by 1784, was completed in 1792. It was surrounded by a moat and a casemate battery in the form of an arch, embracing the enclave. Levelled and concreted in the late 19th Century, the fort housed, at the time, casemate batteries armed with 27cm then 32cm guns, covering the channel approach, together with an open-air battery with six 32cm guns facing out to sea. Only the foundations and the 18th Century entrance facade remain, including a colossal yet extremely elegant gate.

The fort interior is a Dantesque maze of galleries, seven metres high, equipped, in particular, with two electric power stations and goods lifts. The galleries also have narrow rails to transport ammunition. During its modernisation in the late 19th Century, the fort was endowed with a small port of distress, protected by two stone groynes, in complement to the curved sloping jetty, paved with granite and offering access to the fort entrance.

Pelee Island fort's immense entrance gate.

Pelee Island, similar to many other islands, also served as a prison during different periods of its history: during the French Revolution, then in 1848, and finally after the Insurrection of the Paris Commune.

Henceforth deserted and of prohibited access, the island remains one of the finest testimonies of the fortification of Cherbourg's roadstead.

Tatihou, a museum island

On the east coast of the Cotentin peninsula, the island of Tatihou covers a surface area of 28 hectares and is located 1,400 metres from the Saint-Vaast shoreline, as the crow files. So how do you get there? In fact, all you need to do is to wait for the tide to go out. A stoned pathway leads to the island, zigzagging its way through the old oyster farm, today covered with "tables" upon which bags are placed, within which the oysters grow. And if you are impartial to walking along the foreshore, two wheeled amphibious boats also provide regular links to the island's small harbour, both at high and low tide.

One of the amphibious boats providing links to Tatihou.

Bordered by rocks on all sides, Tatihou's granite reefs extend southwards over a distance of approximately 1.5 miles. The island has been protected from seaward invasion by stone seawalls, flanking its three most vulnerable sides. One hundred metres to the south of the island, L'Ilet, the neighbouring islet's entire surface is covered by a fortified structure.

The first signs of human settlement on the island of Tatihou date back to 20,000 years BC. However, remnants recovered on the island date essentially from the Bronze Age (5000-1800 years BC): excavation work conducted in 1996, during the creation of a maritime garden, enabled pottery, millstones, oven parts and stone tools to be unearthed, together with traces of land plots and agricultural buildings, hence the island's valuable Bronze Age heritage, renowned throughout Western France.

The Vikings have left their mark on the island through its very name. In old Scandinavian, the *"hou"* of Tatihou, already present in many other of the Channel Island's names (Lihou, Burhou, Ecrehou...), means "land surrounded by water". Then, in the Middle Ages, the island and its surrounding waters proved to offer advantageous landing conditions to the English. Among others, in 1346, Edward III, Philip the Fair's grandson on his mother's side, and self-pronounced King of England and of France, landed there and subsequently ravaged the Cotentin coast before going on to beat the French at Crécy.

In the 16th Century, a manor farm and a tower were occupied for a while by the Catholic Ligueurs.
Further fortification work was conducted in 1628, following fears of an English incursion; however the tower was finally demolished after orders from the King of France

in 1662, with the participation of the Bailiwick of Cotentin parishes, who worked in corves until completion of the demolition work in 1666.

During the last decade of the 17th Century, the La Hougue disaster was to highlight the absolute necessity to fortify both the island and the coastline. Louis XIV had offered to help the Catholic, James II recover the English Crown. A landing operation in England was planned and the French and Irish troops gathered in La Hougue's neighbouring parishes. Vice Admiral Tourville was in command of the French fleet due to cast off from Brest on its way to La Hougue and to escort the ships already anchored there and transporting James II's troops. However this landing operation was finally to be abandoned following heavy French losses before Cherbourg and La Hougue.

The Tatihou tower:

The battles of Barfleur, Cherbourg and La Hougue

A Dutch engraving depicting the Battle of La Hougue.

Tourville took to the English Channel with a fleet of 44 ships. The French fleet was spotted, as already mentioned, by the Guernsey corsair, John Tupper, who immediately alerted the British Admiralty. On the 29th of May 1692, Tourville ran into the English and Dutch fleets off Barfleur, the latter having joined forces and comprising 99 ships of the line. After a first day of combat, more or less in favour of the French, the order to withdraw was hindered by strong currents. On their way to Saint-Malo, the first French vessels succeeded in reaching the Raz Blanchard, at the extremity of the Cotentin headland, before the currents turned. However, the thirteen largest ships, among which Tourville's own vessel, were driven northwards. Pursued by the English, they had no choice but to approach the coast in seek of refuge.

On Sunday the 1st of June, three vessels were destroyed by the English off Cherbourg. Tourville continued his route towards La Hougue, counting on support from the port's existing troops and ships. When he arrived there, although ready and willing to enter into renewed combat, Tourville received orders to beach his vessels. Six of them were therefore beached near the island of Tatihou and a further six behind the La Houge headland. Out to sea, fifty or so enemy ships, along with a hundred long boats, were preparing to attack.

At evening tide on the 2nd of June, seeing the virtually defenceless French vessels, the English were free to open fire, at little risk for their own safety, first of all on those beached near Tatihou. On the morning of the 3rd of June, they continued their dismal task by burning the six other vessels anchored off La Hougue.

In 1694, Benjamin de Combes, the king's engineer and one of Vauban's collaborators, finally received orders to fortify the La Hougue bay by building the La Hougue and the Tatihou towers.

The tower, erected on the south-west of the island of Tatihou, is 21 metres high and 20 metres in diameter, comprising, as does the La Hougue tower, three levels, one of which was essentially used as a gunpowder store and the two others providing soldiers' and officers' accommodation, before themselves being used as gun-

Ilet fort.

Former guardroom and lazaret enclosure.

powder stores in the 19th Century. The tower's upper platform can house ten cannons. The tower is surrounded by an "entrenched farm", comprising barracks, gardens and a chapel.

On the neighbouring island, L'Ilet, a dry stone and turfed redoubt was built. Later, in the 19th Century, it was modernised with the addition of a fortified structure referred to as the "coastal redoubt", intended to accommodate 60 men and according to standard plans adopted in 1846.

A lazaret surrounded by an enclosure and firing holes occupies the island's west coast; it was built in 1723 to ensure the sanitary control of vessels travelling from the Midi and infested with the Plague.
The lazaret's interior houses different buildings appropriate to the enclosure's original function. A fine hospital building, erected in 1822 to satisfy new sanitary regulations, underwent further alterations as from 1888, to house a host laboratory for researchers from the natural history museum, who paid regular visits to Tatihou up to 1923.

In the 19th Century, the Tatihou fort's limited modernisation involved the development of a substantial powder magazine, in service as from 1869 within the entrenched farm, together with the construction of a bastioned redoubt surrounded by a moat.

During World War I, the island was converted into a prison for German and Austrian civilians.

After the museum researchers had left, a holiday camp entitled the *"Ermitage de Tatihou"* and managed by the *Ministère de l'Instruction Publique* (Ministry for Public Education), was set up on the island, welcoming many youngsters from 1926 to World War II. During the Occupation, German troops were posted in the barracks and civilian access to the island was prohibited. Bunkers

One of the German bunkers defending the "entrenched farm".

were built and mines were planted on the island's grassland. After the island's ransacked buildings had been restored, Tatihou was used to house a rehabilitation centre for adolescents. The centre was closed in 1984 and the island's

Many a painting or a testimony of Normandy's maritime history can be seen in the maritime museum.

different buildings were neglected and vandalised.

This situation was to draw the attention of the Manche County Council, whose President, Pierre Aguiton was an extremely cultured man. The Council had the buildings restored and created a remarkable museographical complex, in perfect harmony with the island's natural environment, whilst the island was placed under the auspices of the *Conservatoire du Littoral* (Coastal Conservancy).

In 1992, the Tercentenary anniversary of the Battle of La Hougue, the island was opened to the public and, since then, has welcomed increasing numbers of visitors each year, thanks to its many

curiosities, starting with its maritime museum and its summer folk festival, *"Les Traversées de Tatihou"*, but also an 800m² botanic garden, home to several hundreds of coastal species planted according to their natural environment (dunes, silt, rocks, heath or prairie), and an immense maritime garden. Finally, a 3 hectare ornithological reserve, created at the fort's extremity, welcomes over 150 different species over the seasons.

Tatihou is the only French island where tourism is controlled, its 2 amphibian boats transporting a maximum of 500 visitors each day.

Tatihou is a sanctuary for many bird species.

The Saint-Marcouf Islands, land of seagulls

Who has never, in their childhood innocence, dreamt of discovering an island or becoming its king? Mysteriously poised on the maritime horizon, occasionally disappearing when, by the vagaries of the weather, the dull greyness erases their outline, the Saint-Marcouf Islands are, in my personal opinion, the archetypal Islands. Those irresistibly appealing islands you absolutely need to discover, after having contemplatively observed them from the shore, far from reach. They were my very first islands, my first maritime destination.

Although relatively unfamiliar, apart from to a few local fishermen or sailing enthusiasts, the tiny Saint-Marcouf archipelago, to the south-west of Saint-Vaast-la-Hougue, is the only group of French islands from the French coast to the Belgian border. The archipelago comprises two islands, the Ile du Large (Sea Island) (approximately 250 metres by 130 metres) and the Ile de Terre (Land Island) (a little longer yet narrower) facing the Cotentin coastline, an eternally geostrategic location. Indeed, given its situation, this coast is sheltered from the prevailing westerly winds and swell, remaining easily approachable thanks to its long sandy beaches, devoid of reefs. Hence, over the centuries since the Middle Ages, the incessant English incursions across this portion of coastline.

The islands form the exposed part of a vast high seabed parallel to

The defensive barracks on Ile du Large.

the coast, referred to as the Banc de la Rade, followed by the Banc de Saint-Marcouf. This high seabed stretches beyond the islands, across the Veys Bay, at which point it is referred to as the Banc du Cardonnet.
These reefs are covered with enough water to present no danger to small sailing boats; however the sea can prove to be cruelly unwelcoming, particularly when the cold east and north-easterly winds blow.

A belt of rocks surrounds the best part of the islands, rendering access all the more difficult, particularly for inexperienced seafarers. The most remarkable include

the rocky Ovy plateau, to the north-west of Ile du Large, which is completely covered at high tide, and the Bastin rock, to the west of Ile de Terre, also covered at mid tide. A channel, of a width of approximately 500 metres at high tide, separates the two islands. Navigable at all times, since offering a permanent depth of no less than 2.5 metres, even at the lowest tides, this channel provides an excellent mooring zone, weather permitting.

The Saint-Marcouf Islands were totally deserted before being noticed, in the 6th Century, by St Marcouf (also known as St Marculf), who sought retreat there.

Saint-Marcouf, Ile du Large.

Their name originates from this inaugural visit. St Marcouf, who had evangelised part of the Cotentin and founded the Abbey of Nantus, liked to retire to these islets to devote himself to prayer and mortification. After having contributed to the influence of his abbey, St Marcouf appeared to wish to continue his mission as a preacher, visiting Jersey where he was to meet his future disciple, St Helier.

In the 10th Century, an attempt was made to establish a small chapel on the islands, in memory of St Marcouf, who remained highly popular.
By the late 11th Century, the monks from the Abbey of Cerisy had settled on the island, to remain there till 1424, building a hermitage and a mill. The Cordeliers, who had set-

tled on the island in 1424, saw their tranquillity too frequently troubled by seafarers and other disreputable buccaneers and finally left these now inhospitable waters in 1477 to settle in Valognes. However, in 1660, certain Valognes Cordeliers, seeking to return to a life of asceticism, received permission to return to the islands from the Seigneur of Fontenay and of Saint-Marcouf. But, only eighteen years later, the islands were once more deserted and drew the attention of the King of France's engineers in charge of fortifying the coastline to prevent any attempted invasion by the English.

Indeed, the sheer length of the east coast of the Cotentin, together with the number of men required to man the few coastal redoubts built over the last decades of the 17th Century

considerably curtailed this fortified line's effective resistance against a potential enemy landing. The situation was exacerbated by the fact that the Saint-Marcouf Islands had neither garrison nor fortifications.

In 1777, the king's engineer, Pierre-Jean de Caux, was convinced of the necessity to fortify and occupy the Saint-Marcouf Islands, whilst, *"the height of the terrain is such that no matter from what side or how strongly the wind blows, the little corsairs (English) are always in safety, they are, so to speak, in ambush, and rare are the times when they remain there more than 24 hours without taking a few boats from the River Isigny"*. De Caux, as many of his predecessors, was not always acknowledged and, in 1795, the commission of the second arrondissement, in charge of defending the coast on behalf of the Comité de Salut Public (Committee for Public Safety) judged that the fortification of the islands should only be conducted once peace had been restored!

However the English were far less patient, and on the 4th of July 1795 they landed a troop on the islands and began to fortify them, hence ensuring the control of the Eastern English Channel. Communication between Cherbourg and Le Havre was critically hindered. Coastal fishing boats were occasionally intercepted by an English cruiser anchored immediately off the islands whilst Royalists and Norman Chouans established, thanks to the islands' occupation, active correspondence which was to facilitate their links with the emigrated princes in England.

Count Louis de Frotté stayed several times on the Saint-Marcouf islands, either on his way to England, or on his return to the Continent. During the same period, Abbot Edgewort de Firmont, who had helped the king on his last days and had even accompanied him to the gallows on the 21st of January 1793, was actively wanted by the Republicans and was subsequently looking to leave France. The Abbot made 5 attempts at reaching the Saint-Marcouf Islands in order to make his way to England, the last of which finally met with success.

The *Directoire*, finally concerned about a potential invasion of the Cotentin from this stronghold, decided to launch a powerful fleet to reclaim the islands. On the dawn of the 7th of May 1798, the fleet, sailing from La Hougue, began its attack; however very few vessels actually attempted to land, intimidated by violent enemy cannon fire and bombs from the islands. Only 5 flat-boats and 2 gunboats attempted to reach the shore; an attempt which

The English establishments on the Saint Marcouf Islands, engraving published in London on the 12th of June 1798, recalling the failed French attempt at reclaiming the islands.

was to result in the loss of ten men and a further fifteen wounded. The entire fleet finally withdrew and left the English "king of their castle".

The islands were only returned to France following the Treaty of Amiens, which was signed between France and the United Kingdom on the 18th of May 1802. The First Consul did not make the same mistake as his predecessors and immediately ordered for the islands to be fortified.
On Ile du Large, he had a defensive tower, or circular fort built, 53 metres in diameter and capable of housing considerable weaponry within its 24 upper level bunkers, completed by a terraced artillery platform.

Fortification work continued up to 1866, although the circular fort was completed under the First Empire, over a period of ten years during which, over and above construction labourers, a garrison of up to 500 men resided on the island, commanded by a small military staff. The officers' families were also resident and three births were registered on the islands in 1817.

Simultaneously, plans to level out Ile de Terre were envisaged due to fears that an enemy might establish camp there and gun the defensive tower on Ile du Large. It was only between 1849 and 1858 that the terraced battery was added, a simple earthen epaulement, together with the guardroom, an "1846 style" redoubt to house 60 men and identical to the one built on Tatihou.

The battery guardroom on Ile de Terre.

having inspected the islands, abandoned them since the range of modern guns did not necessitate the site's armament. However, they did not leave the islands without planting mines there.

Immediately prior to the D-Day landings, the Allied Staff, to ensure that the islands were unoccupied, had detachments from the 4th and 24th Cavalry Squadrons, preceded by a commando of four naval frogmen whose mission it was to facilitate their approach.

Although they met with no garrison, the Americans found themselves amidst a genuine minefield, certain mines exploding under their very feet, causing injury and even losses! However, thanks to their great courage, the islands were to become the

Shags.

Of the two Saint-Marcouf Islands, only Ile du Large is equipped with a small harbour and a lighthouse. The small harbour, which replaced the former rudimentary quay, was only developed in 1862 at the same time as the stone enclosure encircling Ile du Large.

Yet, as early as the 1st of November 1840, a fixed lantern had been installed on one of the Ile du Large fort's interior turrets, offering a valuable accompaniment to the lights in the La Hougue bay. During the Occupation, the Germans destroyed the lighthouse and, after very first French territory liberated on the 6th of June 1944, as early as 5.30am. One hour later, the Landings had begun at the "La Madelaine" hamlet on the shores of Utah Beach, before the village of Saint-Marie-du-Mont.

The Saint-Marcouf Islands were demined after the Liberation.

The lighthouse was rebuilt and relit, on the 5th of May 1947, on a new square turret on the tower's terraced roof, the inside granite turret having been reduced to ruins. Today, the lighthouse is electrified via a solar energy system.

However, over the last sixty years, the exceptional heritage offered by Ile du Large's fort, has become increasingly vulnerable to the attacking seas, due to the absence of regular maintenance. Over the years, the islet's tiny harbour has become unsuitable for navigation purposes and its mole and jetty have been destroyed by storms. Cracks have appeared in the remaining seawalls surrounding the island, the others having given way to the violent waves.

Henceforth, the islands offer a pleasant destination for Norman... and also English seafarers during the summer months, remaining deserted the rest of the year. This haven therefore provides an excellent breeding ground for many herring gulls, black-backed and great black-backed gulls which reside there on a permanent basis. The same applies to several other seabird species such as the great cormorant, the shag, the little egret and several hibernating species such as common eiders, razorbills and common murres. The islands also offer an excellent stopping place for a number of migratory birds. Ile de Terre is a protected ornithological reserve since 1967 and landing on the island is strictly forbidden.

And it is upon these tiny isles, also under British rule for around 8 years, that our grand tour of the islands and islets comprising this extraordinary archipelago off the Cotentin coastline comes to a close. For many, all of these islands remain terra incognita. Yet their grey outline on the maritime horizon is a permanent invitation, an insistent temptation towards discovery, travel, adventure... So when will you set sail?

A permanent and insistent temptation.

Eperquerie's ruined tower, Sark.

Bibliography

- *A guide to the Fortifications of Alderney, 1. Pré-Victorian, 2. Victorian, 3. German,* Alderney, Alderney Society, 1980.
- *A guide to Ministerial government in Jersey,* Jersey, States of Jersey, October 2005.
- *An illustrated history of the occupation of Jersey by German Forces 1940- 1945,* Jersey, Sanctuary Inns Limited, 1995.
- **Barros** (Jean), *Les seigneurs de Carteret en Cotentin et dans les îles anglo-normandes,* Carteret, Cercle Généalogique de la Manche, 29th August 1999,
- **Barthélemy** (Guy), *Jersey vieux pays,* Tartonne, Publication du Pélican, 1974.
- **Barthélemy** (Guy), *Les îles Chausey,* Tartonne, Publication du Pélican, 1973.
- **Brett** (C.E.B.), *Buildings in the town and parish of St Peter Port,* Belfast, National Trust of Guernsey, 1975.
- **Brett** (C.E.B.), *Buildings of the island of Alderney,* Belfast, Alderney Society, 1976.
- **Brett** (C.E.B.), *Buildings in the town and parish of Saint Helier,* Belfast, National Trust for Jersey, 1977.
- **Dawes** (Gordon), *Laws of Guernsey,* Oxford, Hart Publishing, 2003.
- **Détrée** (Jean-François), *Tatihou, histoire d'une île,* Saint-Vaast-la-Hougue, Musée maritime de l'île Tatihou, 1993.
- **Détrée** (Jean-François) and **Moebs** (Mathilde), *Découvrir l'îleTatihou,* Saint-Vaast-la-Hougue, Musée maritime de l'île Tatihou, 2003.
- **Canu** (A.-H.), *Histoire des îles de la Manche,* Paris, Charles Bayle, 1892.
- **Coysh** (Victor), *Alderney,* Plimouth, David and Charles Limited, 1974.
- **Coysh** (Victor), *Royal Guernsey,* Guernsey, Guernsey Press Co. Ltd, 1977.
- **Dalido** (Pierre), *Jersey île agricole, île anglo-normande,* Vannes, Imprimerie A. Chaumeron, 1951.
- **Dupont** (Gustave), *Histoire du Cotentin et de ses îles,* Caen, F. Le Blanc-Hardel, Libraire-Éditeur, 1885.
- **Everard** (Judith), « Les îles normandes en 1204 : le rôle décisif de l'aristocratie normande », *1204 La Normandie entre Plantagenets et Capétiens,* Caen, Publications du CRAHM, 2007.
- **Ewen** (H.) and **de Carteret** (Allan R.), *The fief of Sark,* Guernsey, The Guernsey Press Co. Ltd. 1969.
- **Field** (Albert), *Rambler's illustrated Guide to Sark,* Guernsey, Paramount Lithoprint, 1976.
- **Fosse** (Gérard), « Le voyage de Gilles de Gouberville à Aurigny », *Les Cahiers Goubervilliens,* Numéro spécial, June 2006.
- **Fournier** (Gérard) et **Heintz** (André), *Opération "AQUATINT",* Cully, OREP Éditions, 2005. (Also translated into English under the title "If I must die")
- **Frémine** (Charles), *La chanson du pays,* Coutances, Éditions Arnaud-Béllée, 1973.
- **Gibon** (comte de), *Un archipel normand, Les Îles Chausey et leur Histoire,* (réédition), Saint-Malo, Éditions l'Ancre de Marine, 1988.
- **Ginns** (Michael) and **Bryans** (Peter), *German fortifications in Jersey,* St Lawrance, Jersey, Meadowbank, 1978
- **Grimsley** (E. J.),*The Historical Development of the Martello Towers in the Channel Islands,* Guernsey, Sarnian Publications, 1988.
- **Gueret** (Yvonnick & Armel), *The isle of Sark,* Chilly-Mazarin, 1973.
- **Hugo** (Victor), *L'archipel de la Manche,* Paris, Calmann Lévy éditeur, 1883.
- **Hurel** (Claude & Gilbert), *Îles Chausey, Histoire des toponymes,* Saint-Lô, Éditions Aquarelles, 2006.
- **Hurel** (Gilbert), *Les îles Chausey,* Paris, Éditions Francis Van de Velde, 1990.
- **Hurel** (Gilbert), *Carnet de bord, Le « Courrier des îles » dans les Anglo-Normandes,* Saint-Lô, Éditions Aquarelles, 1999.
- *Island of Sark - Test of opinion on composition of the Chief Pleas,* London, Electoral Reform Services, 2006.
- **Jacqueline** (Mgr Bernard), « Sixte IV et la piraterie dans les îles anglo-normandes », *Revue du département de la Manche,* t. 20, 1978.
- **Le Cerf** (Théodore), *Petite histoire des îles normandes,* (réédition de l'ouvrage de 1862), Pau, PyréMonde Princi Negue, 2006.
- *Le Cotentin et les îles de la Manche dans la tourmente 1939-1945,* (Cherbourg), Société Nationale Académique de Cherbourg, 1987.
- **Le Dain** (John), *Jersey Rambles,* Saint-Hélier, Seaflower Books, 2005.
- **Le Maistre** (Dr Frank), *The Language of Auregny,* Jersey, Le Don Balleine and The Alderney Society and Museum, 1982.
- **Lemprière** (Raoul), *Buildings and memorials of the Channel Islands,* London, Robert Hale Limited, 1980.
- **Le Patourel** (John), *Feudal Empires : Norman and Plantagenet,* London, The Hambledon Press, 1984.
- **Le Patourel** (John), « Guernsey, Jersey and their environment in the middle ages », French translation by Jean Deuve, *Revue du département de la Manche,* t. 33, 1991.
- **Machon** (Nick), *Guernsey as it was,* Guernsey, The Guernsey Press Company, (s. d.).

- *Minutes of the meeting held in the Assembly Room*, Michaelmas Chief Pleas, Sark, Government of Sark, Oct. 2006.
- *Minutes of the Mid-Summer meeting of Chief Pleas held in the Assembly Room*, Sark, Government of Sark, July 2007.
- **Moireau** (Fabrice), *L'île de Tatihou*, Gallimard, 1997.
- **Ogier** (Darryl), *The government and law of Guernsey*, Guernsey, States of Guernsey, 2005.
- **Pégot-Ogier** (M.), *Histoire des îles de la Manche*, Paris, E. Plon et Cie, 1881.
- **Poirey** (Sophie), « L'Archipel anglo-normand, 800 ans de contestations franco-anglaise », Colloquium, « *La France et les îles britanniques : un couple impossible ?* », Caen, Sept. 2007, Pending publication.
- **Poirey** (Sophie), « Le droit coutumier à l'épreuve du temps : l'application de la coutume de Normandie dans les îles anglo-normandes à travers l'exemple du retrait lignager », *Revue historique de droit français et étranger (RHD)*, n° 75, p. 377-414.
- **Pouchain** (Gérard), *Promenades dans l'Archipel de la Manche avec un guide nommé Victor Hugo*, Condé-sur-Noireau, Editions Charles Corlet, 1985.
- **Remphry** (Martin), *Sark folklore*, Sark, Gateway Publishing Ltd, 2003.
- **Selosse** (Louis), *L'île de Serck un état féodal au xxe siècle*, Lille, Imprimerie G. Sautai, 1911.
- **Serc** (Patrick), *De Saint-Marcouf à Saint-Malo*, Courtils, Patrick Serc, 2007.
- **Sinsoilliez** (Robert), *Histoire des Minquiers et des Écréhou*, Saint-Malo, L'ancre de Marine, 1995.
- **Sinsoilliez** (Robert), *Les espions du roi*, Louviers, L'ancre de marine, 2006.
- **Tancréde** (Ch.), *La clameur de haro*, Rouen, Les Éditions du Veilleur de Proue, 1999.
- **Thin** (Edmond), *Quand l'ennemi venait de la mer*, Saint-Lô, O.D.A.C., 1992.
- **Thin** (Edmond), *Les îles Saint-Marcouf*, Cully, OREP Éditions, 2005.
- **Thin** (Edmond), *Sentinelles de mer en Cotentin*, Cully, OREP Éditions, 2006.
- **Vercel** (Roger), *Les îles anglo-normandes*, Paris, Albin Michel, 1956.

Creux Harbour, Sark.

Acknowledgements

It is with great pleasure that the author addresses his sincere thanks to all who have offered their precious contribution, and in particular, the following:

▥ Marine Nationale, Préfecture maritime Manche-Mer du Nord: Lieutenant *Yann Bizien* and the *CPAR, Cherbourg*, for his superb aerial picutres,

▥ *Mr Gilles Désiré dit Gosset*, director of the Manche heritage department, and his colleagues for their efficient help and their receptiveness,

▥ *Mr Nicolas Buanic*, curator of the Navy Historical Defence Department in Cherbourg, and *Mr. François Zoonkindt*,

▥ *Mrs Sophie Poirey-Boutin* for her great knowledge of the islands' customs and institutions,

▥ *Mr Jean-François Détrée*, director of the Tatihou Maritime Museum, and *Mrs Mathilde Moebs*,

▥ *Mrs Geneviève Thin* and *Laure Thin*,

▥ *Mrs Gabrielle Guéret* for her kind permission to use *Mr Yvonnic Guéret's* (†) magnificent aerial photographs,

▥ *Mr Rémi Conan, Mr Gérard Debout, Mr Bertrand Sciboz and Mr Robert Sinsoilliez*, who kindly allowed us to use some of their photographs,

▥ The directors and curators of a number of museums and tourist offices, together with the inhabitants of Alderney, Guernsey, Sark and Jersey who considerably facilitated our research on the islands.

▥ *Mr Gérard Grimbert*, for his meticulous rereading of the texts and proofs, together with *Mr Philippe Mareuil*,

▥ *Mrs Sophie Youf*, for her lovely layout and graphic design, and the entire team at *OREP*.

Illustrations

Illustrations have essentially been provided by the author from his personal collection, with the exception of the following:

▥ **Manche County Archives:** 4, 8, 13 b, 26 t, 37 t, 39 b, 81 b, 94 l, 113 b, 118, 128 t, 171 br.

▥ **French Navy, CPAR, Cherbourg:** 153, 154 t, 155, 156 b, 157 t.

▥ **Tatihou Maritime Museum:** 180 t.

▥ **Navy Historical Defence Department in Cherbourg:** 177 b.

▥ **Jersey Tourism, Image library:** 10, 64 t, 114, 129 b, 140 tr, 142, 143 b, 146 b.

▥ **States of Alderney, Image gallery:** 14 t (Ilona Soane-Sands), 23, 29 t, 31, 36 bl and br.

▥ **States of Guernsey, Tourist Board:** 6, 12, 35, 43, 46, 49, 53 d, 59 g, 57 tr, 60 except tr, 61 t, 61 l, 62 t, 63 r, 65 r, 67, 70 b, 72 b, 73, 75 b, 78, 79, inside cover flap, back cover flap, back cover centre.

▥ **Personal collections:** 120 t, 127 l, 185 l.

▥ **Rémi Conan:** 170, 174.

▥ **Gérard Debout – GONm:** 186 b.

▥ **Yvonnick Guéret:** Front cover top, 37 c, 154 b, 157 b, 158, 161, 184

▥ **Bertrand Sciboz:** 15 t.

▥ **Robert Sinsoilliez:** 160, 164.

▥ **Laure Thin:** 100 cr.

Front cover:
The Minquiers' Maîtr'Ile.
Inserts, from left to right: Castle Cornet in Guernsey. Alderney Lighthouse.
Le Hocq Point Tower on Jersey.

Back cover, successively: Returning to Sark after a fishing trip. Alderney telephone box and letter box. The midday salute at Castle Cornet, Guernsey. *"Ruette Tranquille"* (peacefull pathway) signpost in Guernsey, signifying priority to riders, cyclists or walkers. Houmet Herbe fort on Alderney. Horse-drawn carriage on Sark. *« La Vaque dé Jèrri »*, monument built in 2001 in St Helier (Jersey), to commemorate the island's renowned Jersey cows. Grande Greve on Sark.

OREP
EDITIONS

15, rue de Largerie - 14480 Cully
Tel: 02 31 08 31 08
Fax: 02 31 08 31 09
E-mail: info@orep-pub.com
Website: www.orep-pub.com

Editor: Philippe Pique
Editorial assistant: Nelly Jennin
Graphic design and layout: Sophie Youf
English translation: Heather Costil

ISBN: 978-2-915762-66-2
First edition: 3rd quarter 2008
Copyright OREP
All rights reserved

Legal deposit: 3rd quarter 2008

Printed in France

Published with support from the Manche County Council, the Lower Normandy Regional Council and the Centre régional des Lettres de Basse-Normandie.